I0633437

the gospel according to dance:
choreography and the bible
from ballet to modern
by the editors of
dance magazine
with text by giora manor

PROPERTY OF

St. Martin's Press, New York

Copyright © 1980 by Danad Publishing Company, Inc. All rights reserved. Portions of this book originally appeared in *Dance Magazine*, December 1978, under the title "The Bible as Dance." No part of this book may be reproduced or transmitted in any form or by any means, electronic or mechanical, including photocopying, recording, or by any information storage and retrieval system, without permission in writing from the Publisher. For information, write: St. Martin's Press, Inc., 175 Fifth Avenue, New York, N.Y. 10010. Manufactured in the United States of America.

Main entry under title:
The Gospel according to Dance.
    1. Religious dance, Modern. I. Manor, Giora.
II. Dance Magazine.
GV1783.5.G67   793.3′2   80-15694
ISBN 0-312-34052-4

GV
1783.5
.G67

the gospel according to dance:
choreography and the bible
from ballet to modern
by the editors of
dance magazine
with text by giora manor

PROPERTY OF

St. Martin's Press, New York

Copyright © 1980 by Danad Publishing Company, Inc. All rights
reserved. Portions of this book originally appeared in *Dance
Magazine*, December 1978, under the title "The Bible as Dance."
No part of this book may be reproduced or transmitted in any
form or by any means, electronic or mechanical, including
photocopying, recording, or by any information storage and
retrieval system, without permission in writing from the
Publisher. For information, write: St. Martin's Press, Inc., 175
Fifth Avenue, New York, N.Y. 10010. Manufactured in the
United States of America.

Main entry under title:

The Gospel according to Dance.

    1. **Religious dance, Modern.**   I.   **Manor, Giora.**
II. Dance Magazine.
GV1783.5.G67   793.3′2   80-15694
ISBN 0-312-34052-4

GV
1783.5
.G67

the gospel according to dance

table of contents

The José Limón Dance Company in Limón's 1956 work, There Is a Time, based on quotations from the Book of Ecclesiastes which begin: "To everything there is a season, and a time to every purpose under the heaven." (Ecclesiastes 3:1)

Members of the Martha Graham Dance Company in the premiere of Graham's **Embattled Garden** *on March 3, 1958. (Photo: Martha Swope)*

preface

When I set out to research Biblical themes in dance (a study precipitated by the then-upcoming international seminar, The Bible in Dance — which took place as scheduled in Jerusalem in August 1979), I was unaware of the scope of my endeavor. Because my task was to be a thematical survey, I had to deal with dance dramaturgy, an aspect of dance which has been neglected lately.

Although many regard dramatic dance as being less "pure" than abstract movement, I do not subscribe to this point of view. I do not quite know, in fact, what "purity" in the arts actually means. The term carries a moral judgment which I find irrelevant to artistic technique and misleading in forming an opinion about the social relevance of works of art.

There appears to exist a dialectic development traceable in all art forms: The pendulum swings from a peak of incorporation and appropriation of means of expression from different disciplines into one in order to enrich and deepen the impact on the audience, to the other extreme of separation, of austerity, of "purification," of exclusion of "alien" devices, for the same reason.

In ballet history these trends are clear. The *ballet de cour* (court ballet) was a mixture of dance, acting, and declamation. Ballet developed toward more abstract forms until the libretto dwindled to a pretext; then there was a rediscovery of fable and drama during the Romantic period, and finally, another swing toward the abstract which led to the plotless ballet of modern times.

A similar swing between the abstract and the dramatic can be seen in the development of modern dance. At present we are experiencing a phase in which acting, the spoken word, and even the tactile experience of the dance spectator are again in vogue.

The Bible, universally accepted as a basic part of Western culture, provides us with an excellent yardstick with which to measure this development and through which to study dance dramaturgy. This aspect is the most relevant one in the following study.

Giora Manor
Mishmar Haemak
September 1979

the bible as dance

As I sit writing, spring clouds are sailing over Nazareth across the valley. The sun makes the green of the fields even deeper. The gray rocks of the Gilboa Mountains are stark bare, as if the curse "Let there be no dew, neither let there be rain upon you" (2 Samuel 1:21), uttered in despair by David upon hearing that King Saul and his own beloved friend Jonathan had fallen in battle, was still valid and powerful today.

A bit further to the north, between Nazareth and Gilboa, lies Ein Dor, where the troubled Saul consulted the witch, and a few miles to the west lies the village of Cana, scene of Christ's first miracle, the turning of water into wine at a wedding feast. Perhaps even today a marriage is being celebrated to the sound of reed-flute and drum (or a tape recorder playing a catchy pop tune).

Should I look westward, I would see the now nearly dry River Kishon, in which General Sisera and his iron war chariots drowned, and a bit further to the west is the place where Jael offered the fleeing general milk, though he asked only for water, and then killed him with a tent peg.

What is remarkable about all this local geography is that there is no need for me to explain the significance of all these places, these persons, and the historical or mythological contexts of these events, even to readers living thousands of miles away from here. Not to those born in the Western Hemisphere, where at least to some extent the Bible, whether Old or New Testament, forms an underpinning of the general culture heritage. The Bible, along with Greek mythology, is the common denominator of Western culture. This general knowledge or familiarity often has little or nothing to do with religious belief.

The events just mentioned, and the places where they occurred, all have been featured in ballets

*Letitia Ide and José Limón in Limón's **The Exiles** (1950), a duet based on the story of Adam and Eve after their expulsion from the Garden of Eden. (Photo: Arnold Eagle)*

based on Biblical subjects. The variety and number of such ballets lend themselves to a survey of the subject, quite apart from the question of what the dancing frequently mentioned in the Bible itself was like, which has been explored by several scholars.

In the year 1462 King René of Provence organized for the Corpus Christi festival a choreographic procession called the Lou Gue, in which the dancers did the *Minuet of the Queen of Sheba* coming to visit King Solomon; another dance depicted Jesus bearing the cross (to King René's own music and choreography); in still another, "Jews were dancing 'round the Golden Calf"; and even the massacre of the Innocents at Bethlehem found saltatory expression in the festive event.

Of course, occasional Biblical dances may be found in many manuscripts of medieval Mysteriums and Passion Plays: Mary Magdalene, sinfully dancing with demons (Mons, 1501) or Salome entertaining Herod and his court, a dance scene we will encounter many times in our survey. Two hundred years after the Lou Gue we find a wealth of Biblical ballets at the end-of-term performances in the schools founded by the Jesuits all over Europe and in South America. These school shows incorporated all of the then-novel elements of stagecraft of the ballet de cour, which flourished at the court of the kings of France since Louis XIV, whose sobriquet *Roi Soleil* was itself but the name of a role he danced in a ballet. The Jesuit educators used the Bible as a source for their plays, in which Joseph in Egypt, Jephthah and his daughter, Abraham sacrificing Isaac, as well as Christ and the Apostles, Lazarus risen from the dead, and many others provided drama, song, and ballet. After the Baroque *Ballett de College* of the Jesuit schools waned, nearly three centuries passed in which the gods of Olympus reigned supreme on the ballet stage and Biblical subjects disappeared altogether, perhaps because these were deemed too sacred for such a secular, not to say profane or even "immoral," art as dance.

The only *ballet de cour* libertto based on the Bible which I have come across is *Le Balet* [sic] *de la Tour de Babel,* published by Paul Lacroix in 1688 in his book *Ballets de Mascarades de Cour de Henri III à Louis XIV, 1581-1652.* The plot involves Nembrot, king of the Assyrians, who is "dissatisfied with his earthly empire," and "decrees a tower be built towards heaven." Workers, masons, architects, "aux dames" and their "maîtresses" take part in the dancing. The ballet turns out to be rather patriotic. After the confusion of languages, "as was prophesied by the Sibyl," all the world will again be

A deeply spiritual José Limón, seen here in a biographical photo taken in his home in 1957, created a number of works based on Biblical themes. (Photo: Anatole Heller)

united and dominated by one tongue alone — the French, naturally.

Language, not in itself a natural subject matter for dance, in this instance supplied the ballet with a traditional balletic device, namely an opportunity to execute different national folk dances, arranged to fit the court style. Apart from the dances of the masons, laborers, and architects, there were Tartars, Spaniards, and, of course, "les cavaliers français aux dames" and the ubiquitous shepherds and shepherdesses of the *ballet de cour*.

God himself does not appear. His verdict is represented by the Sibylline prophecy. The story touches on the Greek principle of hubris, the pride of mortals resulting in their own downfall. The Biblical theme is used as a pretext for a patriotic ballet.

With the advent of modern dance at the turn of the twentieth century, choreographers again turned to the Bible for inspiration, and since then there hardly exists a dance creator who has not tried his hand at Biblical ballets.

In 1895, for example, Loie Fuller's shimmering veils, which made her famous, quite naturally became Salome's seven veils. A few years later, in 1911, she danced *Miriam's Dance* (about the triumphant crossing of the Red Sea by the Israelites leaving Egyptian bondage), and in 1921 added to her repertoire a dance titled *The Deluge* — her veils in both cases representing the waters.

At the turn of the century Salome and her passion for Jokanaan's (John the Baptist's) red lips became notorious due to Oscar Wilde's one-act play. Maude Allan, another American pioneer of modern dance, created quite a scandal with her *Vision of Salome,* which she performed in Europe in 1907, arousing the wrath of censors and getting herself involved with the authorities in Germany and England because of her daring costume, which consisted only of strings of pearls forming a bra and loincloth.

Ruth St. Denis danced her version of Salome as late as 1948, but in 1918 had already done *Jephthah's Daughter,* and one year later *Dancer at the Court of King Ahasuerus* (Esther). Ted Shawn danced *Joseph's Legend* in 1915 and created his *Miriam, Sister of Moses* in 1919 and *The Twenty-third Psalm* two years later.

Miriam, Sister of Moses was produced in California in 1919 as a full-length play with dance; Miriam was played and danced by Ruth St. Denis, Shawn creating the choreography. The text was by Maxwell and Constance Armfield. The role of Moses was danced by Shawn. "The part of Miriam was wholly conceived and played in the light of dance technique. In long textual passages, brief

Pauline Koner as The Iniquitous One and Robert Walton as The Prophet in Koner's Voice in the Wilderness *(1948), a work based on texts from Isaiah. (Photo: John Lindquist)*

moments of reflection or rapid utterance and sweeping movements across the stage, St. Denis never acted but ever danced, showing always a rhythmic affection for the situation." This is how F. McConnell described the show in *Theatre Arts Magazine*, October 1919.

"Dances, after the Japanese tradition, when the speaker reaches a white heat of emotion. Psalms, Choruses and Processionals for the highest points of exaltation. The movement throughout the play is of great importance." Thus Armfield describes the style of the play in his notes.

A special color scheme was devised to portray the characters. "The rabble stream across the scene at the opening in dark grays and reds with flickers of paler gray, the dawn being indicated by gradual introduction of smoky orange and golden dresses, which constantly lighten and intensify until the final flame of Miriam and her maidens in flame-color and spark-like metallic gold. Moses seemed necessarily white throughout; Joshua introduced a blue note, and the rebels were characterized by purple, dark gray with lush greens as a border, and dark-speckled pale gray prefigures the sulphurous and electric color of the Golden Calf episode." Thus the author describes his intentions and one is reminded of the painted bodies of the dancers in Kassian Goleizovsky's *Joseph the Beautiful,* staged several years later in Moscow, a device which, together with the other innovations the choreographer introduced, scandalized the Soviet authorities.

All his life Shawn was passionately interested in the relationship between dance and religion and returned to Biblical themes when he choreographed his *Job, a Masque for Dancing,* in 1931,

Ruth St. Denis and Ted Shawn pose in two scenes from Miriam, Sister of Moses, *a Biblical "drama" with choreography by Shawn for himself and St. Denis; performed at the Greek Theatre, University of California, Berkeley, 1919. (Photo: Korajewski, Dance Collection, Library and Museum of Performing Arts)*

coincidentally the same year as Ninette de Valois created her *Job* to music by Ralph Vaughan Williams for the Camargo Society in London (recently given new choreography as a television show by Robert Cohan). Other Biblical dances by Ted Shawn were *Dreams of Jacob* (1949) and *Song of Songs* (1951).

The list of modern choreographers inspired by the Bible is a long one. To name but a few: Martha Graham, José Limón, Lester Horton, Harald Kreutzberg, Glen Tetley, Charles Weidman, Norman Walker, Anna Sokolow, and Serge Lifar; Aurel von Milloss and John Neumeier in the classical ballet sphere.

After classical ballet had neglected, or rather did not dare to tackle, Biblical subjects for nearly three hundred years, they were reintroduced in the twentieth century when Michel Fokine created *Josephslegende* (to music by Richard Strauss) for Diaghilev in 1914. Ten years later the Soviet choreographer Kassian Goleizovsky presented his *Salome* (music by Richard Strauss) and a year later shocked Moscow audiences with his innovative *Joseph the Beautiful.* One of Balanchine's outstanding ballets, *The Prodigal Son,* was the last work presented by Diaghilev before his death in 1929. Balanchine prepared another version of his *Prodigal* in Copenhagen in 1931 and later, in America, created *Samson and Delilah* and *Noah and the Flood* for television in 1962.

As early as 1923 Jean Börlin choreographed Milhaud's *Creation of the World* for the Swedish Ballet, another Biblical legend which keeps attracting choreographers, even those as far from religious beliefs as Natalia Kasatkina and Vladimir Vasiliev, who used Jean Effel's cartoons for their *Creation* for the Kirov Ballet in Leningrad in 1971. The

One of Hollywood's most famous Salomes, Rita Hayworth, performs two scenes from the "Dance of the Seven Veils" in the film Salome, *released by Columbia Pictures in the early 1950s.*

Martha Graham and May O'Donnell (right) in Graham's Herodiade (1944), created to the music of Hindemith, with a set designed by Isamu Noguchi.

panorama of Biblical ballet is vast, unconfined to any one concept or philosophy. Everyone finds in "The Good Book" what he is looking for.

For the inventors of modern dance, it possessed the exotic flavor required by Fuller's, St. Denis's, or Allan's solos. For Graham, the Bible provides the monumental mythical structures around which she builds her psychological dramas.

The rich dramatic Biblical situations supply some choreographers with ready-made scaffolds upon which to erect their dances. For others the Psalms or the Book of Job are the means to convey philosophical thought in terms abstract, yet concrete enough to accommodate dance, the most physical of art forms, in which the sensual and spiritual meet. Majestic tragedy — mankind cast out of the bliss of Eden, brother killing brother, sinning humanity threatened by destruction by flood; towering figures such as the patriarch Jacob struggling with the Angel, and Abraham about to sacrifice his own son; epic tales of blood and death — David vanquishing Goliath and leading his people to victory, Moses leading his nation from slavery to freedom; success stories — Joseph, sold into captivity by his brothers, becoming viceroy of Egypt, and Esther, the unknown girl, becoming queen and rescuing her people from a "final solution"; passion leading to betrayal and tragic blindness and revenge — Samson and Delilah; pure bucolic love in the Song of Songs, and a love as unconventional as David's for Jonathan; betrayed friendship — Judas's kiss; the dead returning to life — Lazarus and, of course, Christ himself; moral tales — the Prodigal Son's return; intrigue — Uriah's wife. It's all there.

Rudolf Nureyev in Martha Graham's Lucifer *(1975). The program notes at the premiere included the following comments: "'How art thou fallen from the heaven, O Lucifer, son of the morning!' — Isaiah 14:12. The name 'Lucifer' means 'fringes of light'; when Lucifer falls from heaven — the state of grace — he who was once a god becomes half-god and half-man. As such he is subject to the fears and passions of man. This is a retelling of a mythical experience which is common to all mankind." (Photo: Martha Swope)*

An unparalleled tapestry of humanity is provided by that ancient anthology which is the Bible and the apocrypha which, I believe, should be considered as one in the present survey. What makes the Old Testament so fascinating to the nonreligious, and so compatible with modern ways of thought, is, I am quite sure, the tolerance of the ancient editors, who did not censor nor delete offending passages, but rather made their opinions clear by adding comment. So the Bible includes records of events which cast a shadow on the reputation of sacred and revered personages, and celebrated heroes are presented with all their warts, making them human and very modern indeed.

Only on the subject of monotheism were the compilers strictly enforcing the dogma. They strove to reconcile the ancient polytheistic sources with their own picture of a world created and dominated by one god alone. While suppressing the polytheistic ideas, they still left intact all the references to the continuing worship of pagan deities, only adding their disapproval.

The New Testament, on the other hand, is not an "official record" at all, but rather a collection of evidence from various sources. Thus, juxtaposed as in a newspaper, one finds in the Bible editorials, chronicles, poetry, and fiction; tales of passion and crime, victory and defeat, love and lust, cruelty and kindness — a portrait of mankind.

Tony Catanzaro in the Boston Ballet's 1977 production of Norman Walker's Lazarus (1973). (Photo: A. Epstein)

Gelee's mezzotint engraving of a Bourdet drawing which depicts the resurrection of Lazarus, one of the miracles from the Bible. (The Bettmann Archive)

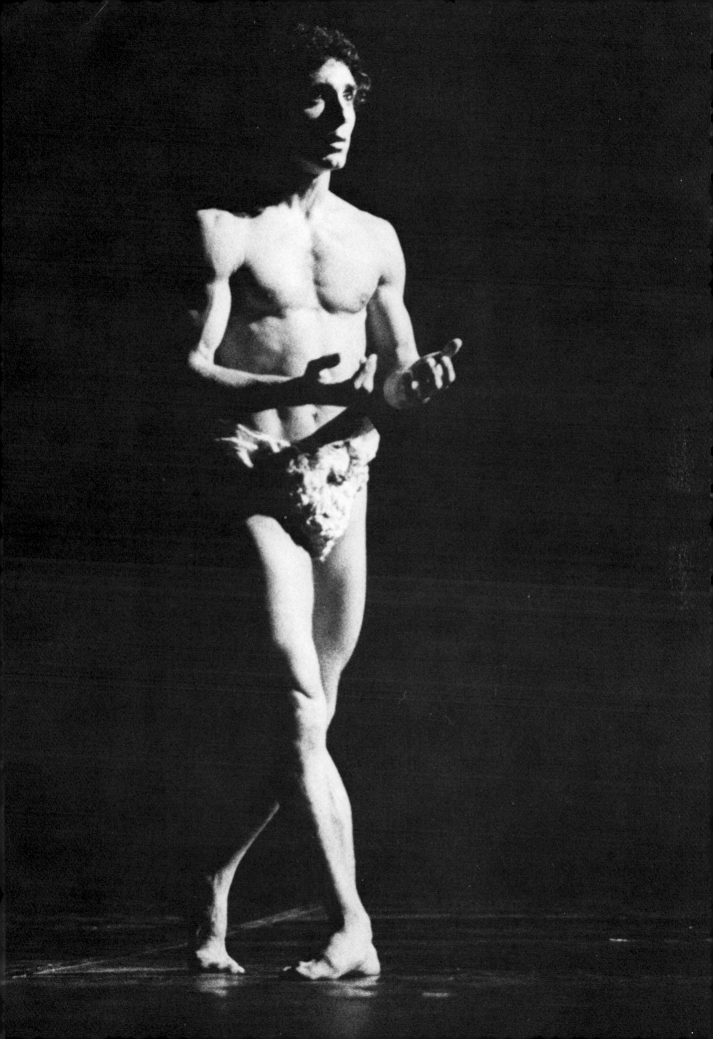

jesuit biblical ballet

When Ignatius of Loyola founded the *Compania de Jesus* in the sixteenth century, education became one of the main tools of the Jesuit order. All over Europe (and at their missions in the New World as well), Jesuit schools employed the theatrical stage as an educational tool, and the staging of drama and spectacles became a means of indoctrination as well as a didactical method for the teaching of Latin and rhetoric. In Jesuit drama the emphasis was on the theatrical, visual aspect of the performances, and so music and dance quickly became an important component. Many of the dramas were based on Biblical subjects. Among these early plays were *Nebuchadnezzar*, *Goliath*, and *Juditha*. The plays, performed by the pupils in Latin, were accompanied by printed programs distributed to the audience, summarizing the plot in the vernacular. In these synopses, called *periochae*, ballet scenes are described. Termed *drama mutum* ("silent play"), the scene is often of an abstract nature, the dancers personifying the virtues or vices evoked in the Biblical or mythological spoken scenes. *Entretenimentes de musica y danza* accompanied the *tragicomedia* of *Joseph* at Ocana in Spain in 1558.

Copper engraving of David slaying Goliath with sling and stone. (The Bettmann Archive)

Ted Shawn in his Dance David the King (1919-20) projected dance work which was never completed. (Photo: Dance Collection, Library and Museum of Performing Arts)

The allegorical ballet interludes provided an interpretation of the Biblical story. For example, the tragedy about the fall of the Assyrian Empire and the prophet Daniel included a ballet called *Les Songes* ("Dreams"), because Nebuchadnezzar the king saw his downfall predicted in a dream.

Dreams occur, quite appropriately, in *Joseph, Viceroy of Egypt* (Paris, 1699), as described by Père Gabriel Le Jay in his *Bibliotheca Rhetorum* (Paris, 1725). The four ballet interludes are as follows: The first depicts the four human temperaments; in the second, "human ambitions lend support to dreams"; the third, in a Freudian vein, is about "passions keeping our dreams alive," in which the dramatis personae are from the Greek *Iliad;* in the final interlude, which is allegorical, Joseph's triumph over his enemies is celebrated by Truth dancing a solo, assisted by Light, vanquishing the Vanities of human reveries.

Several of the Biblical dramas included dances as an integral part of the plot itself, such as *Jephthah's Daughter,* staged by the Jesuit students at Ingolstadt, Germany, in 1637, or another version produced in

Adam and Eve, *a painting by Lucas Cranach the Elder (1472-1553). (The Bettmann Archive)*

Dennis Wayne and Starr Danias in the Joffrey Ballet's production of Jo Butler's After Eden *(1966 (Photo: Herb Migdoll)*

John Butler's **In the Beginning** *(1959), danced by members of the Metropolitan Opera Ballet: Sondra Lee (on shoulders), Thomas Andrew, Bambi Linn, and Bruce Marks (kneeling). (Photo: Warman)*

David Rapoport, Jeannet[t]e Ordman, and Igal Berdichevsky in the Bat-Dor Dance Company produc-tion of John Butler's Acc[or]-ding to Eve (1972), a wor[k] which deals with the stor[y] of Cain and Abel as seen through the eyes of their mother, Eve. (Photo: Mu[l] & Haramaty)

Belgium, written by Luminaeus a Marca, in 1613. The story (Judges 11:34) has Jephthah's daughter dancing out to welcome her father returning victorious from battle, unaware that his vow has condemned her, as the first to meet him on his return, to be "sacrificed" (not as a human sacrifice, but by taking vows of chastity and celibacy). The staging was often very modern in concept, the fateful meeting between Jephthah and his daughter taking place by torchlight or, in 1755 at Hildesheim, Germany, followed by an allegorical dance between the heroine and Death.

The ballets became elaborate affairs, sometimes more than fifty dancers participating. Stage machines were in use, and there exist several decrees by church authorities limiting the size of the productions and only grudgingly allowing the playing of female roles by the schoolboys. As ballet masters, the Jesuit fathers would often invite artists of court ballet companies to stage their shows.

The performances became very popular. In Vienna a courtyard of the school was covered by a roof to create a theater and Jean Loret records that, in France, King Louis XIV himself attended Jesuit Biblical ballets and witnessed "the pleasureful dances, ballets, postures and cadences." The boys excelled in the art of dance and acrobatic movement, as is clear from the copperplate of a sword dance of *Hester* (Esther) from Munich or from records of an ecstatic dance of shepherds celebrating the patriarch Jacob's blessing.

The allegory involved in Jesuit Biblical ballet was sometimes twofold, the Biblical story being used to celebrate a contemporary event. Thus Nicolaus Avancini's *Joseph* was staged in Vienna in 1650 as a peace celebration; *Cyrus*, at the betrothal of Leopold of Austria in 1673; in the 1642 play *Judith*, the general Holofernes represented the commanding officer of the invading Swedish armies; in Russia, at the court of Peter I, after his victory at Poltava (1703), *The Divine Humbling of the Proud Conquerors, depicted as the Vanishing of Goliath, the Proud Conqueror, by the Humble David, with Ballet and Music* was performed. Ironically enough, *Humble David* was to represent Russia in this allegory. On the other hand, the use of allegory enabled the Jesuit Fathers to overcome the problem of depicting sacred personages on stage in dance, an art always regarded as suspiciously profane. Often the ballet interludes interpolated in the Biblical play used a pagan, usually Greek, myth to render the story in a kind of analogy. The poet Jacob Balde (Germany, 1604-1668) points out in his *Jephtias* that the sacrificing of the daughter is, in fact, an allegory of the martyr's death of Christ as the Son of

Paul Taylor and membe of his company in "Wes Eden," the second part Taylor's American Gene (1973). (Photo: Kenn Duncan)

God, and that he used the legend of Iphigenia for the dance scenes to create this multilayered allegory. Subtle dramatic irony pervades the scene in which the maidens dance, welcoming Jephthah. As the joyous dance takes place, a trumpet sounds from afar, constantly coming nearer, heralding the fateful approach of the conquering hero, which brings tragedy to the celebrants.

Another example of allegory in treatment of Biblical themes may be found in *Abraham against God and Isaac against his Obedience of his Father,* performed in Austria in 1725.

The work starts with a dance in which mermaids tell Cassiopeia that because of her excessive pride she is commanded to throw her daughter Andromeda into the sea, where she will be devoured by a whale. She is handed over to Mercury to be bound to a rock at the seashore. Then the Biblical story commences, to be interrupted again by ballet, after Sarah's lament of her son's fate. The interlude shows the heroine being bound by Mercury to the rock "as the whale's jaws threaten to swallow her."

Abraham returns, and the sacrifice of Isaac is prepared until God's angel interferes and strikes the knife from Abraham's raised hand at the last moment.

The show ends with another ballet scene, in which Perseus releases Andromeda, taking her away with him to be his bride, "all done for the greater glory of God."

creation

Why did God bother with the Creation in the first place? Why this whole complex game with its intricate rules granting man the choice between good and evil but reserving the final arbitration of His creatures' fate for Himself? Perhaps God was simply bored with His infinite, perfect, absolute void?

Indeed, several choreographers have indicated in their respective "creation" ballets that the beginning of mankind was a sort of joke. Sometimes the smile is a rather lopsided one, as the joke is at our expense. But man's loss of eternal bliss, his being condemned to toil without joy by the sweat of his brow all of his life, the murder of a brother, these and similar situations indicate real tragedy; and there are choreographers who have treated Genesis in this deadly serious way. Both viewpoints seem theatrically valid, since what is deemed funny or sad is determined by the interpreter, not by the material itself.

To choose a few examples from the many modern dances about Genesis, let us consider first some well-known ones: José Limón's *Exiles,* John

Robert Cohan and Matt Turney, as the Stranger and Lilith, in Martha Graham's Embattled Garden. (Photo: Martha Swope)

Martha Graham's 1958 E battled Garden deals wit the story of Adam and E before their expulsion fr the Garden of Eden. See in the work here are (left right) Paul Taylor, Mary Hinkson, Bertram Ross, and Matt Turney. (Photo Martha Swope)

"... the screech owl [Lilith] also shall rest the and find for herself a pla of rest." (Isaiah 34:14)

Bertram Ross and Yurik as Adam and Eve, in Graham's Embattled Garden.

Butler's *After Eden,* and Martha Graham's *Embattled Garden.* Both duets — Limón's and Butler's — begin with the protagonists already expelled from Eden, and now wandering in a barren, inhospitable wilderness. In both, Adam and Eve are strangers in the world outside the Garden of Eden.

They are becoming acquainted with the human predicament; they are groping for an emotional foothold, searching for their identity, and finding each other. Their partnership is the only real hope in the situation in which they find themselves. This companionship is the only possible solace in the solitude and isolation of man deprived of the eternal bliss of Eden.

The very emptiness of the stage lends the necessary atmosphere, and when, for example, *After Eden* was produced by the Harkness Ballet in 1968 with sets by Rouben Ter-Arutunian, Marcia Siegel found it "like objets trouvés from a giant's auto parts store . . . purely decorative, although not pretty."

Both these works treat the *Paradise Lost* situation, while the Graham ballet, *Embattled Garden,* deals with the time prior to the expulsion. Here the Garden of Eden is the garden of love. The Stranger, representing the Biblical serpent, brings unrest into the tranquillity of Eden. He perches high on a stylized tree, stage left (set by Isamu Noguchi), watching the other three characters at peace among the reeds on the opposite side of the stage. Graham introduces a fourth character, in addition to the Stranger, Adam, and Eve: Lilith, an evil spirit or demon who, according to Jewish legend, was Adam's spouse before the creation of Eve.

Lilith also figures in Joel Schnee's ballet, *Moses, Jeremiah, Solomon, David und Viele Andere* (" . . . and many others"), premiered at Kassel, West Germany, in 1977, which is a spoof on Biblical

*Ohad Naharin and Tamar Zafrir in the Batsheva Dance Company production of Oshra Elkayam-Ronen's **Adam and Eve.** (Photo: Jaacov Agor)*

Todd Bolender's 1961 ballet, Creation of the World. (Photo: Martha Swope)

stories. The program notes include a *Midrash*, a medieval Hebrew commentary, which seeks to explain why the relationship between Lilith and Adam was an unhappy one, and why God had to find a better solution for Adam's marital life. While he was formed from clean clay, the commentary explains, Lilith was molded from dirty mud, and so she became recalcitrant and quarrelsome, and refused to "lie beneath him" when they made love. So God was more careful when He created Eve, from Adam's own rib, and he braided her beautiful hair and embellished it with precious stones and pearls before presenting her to Adam.

Graham's *Embattled Garden* elevates the Biblical situation to an abstract level, not bothering at all with telling the story itself, which one may safely suppose everyone knows. It is the strange alchemy of love which attracts Graham's interest. "Love, it has been said, does not obey the rules of love, but some more ancient and ruder law. The Garden of Love seems always to be threatened by the Stranger's knowledge of those like Lilith, who lived there first," say the program notes.

The figure of God Himself is absent from all three works considered above. How to present God on stage has been a problem for producers and choreographers even in fairly recent times, the taboo being an ancient one often embedded in common law. Thus, when Ninette de Valois created her *Job* in 1931, God had to be called "Job's Spiritual Self" to overcome the objections of The Lord Chamberlain, who acted as censor in Britain until about fifteen years ago.

No such problem was encountered by de Valois when she choreographed her *Création du Monde* in 1931, as in this version of Genesis there appear three African deities. Darius Milhaud called his

Sara Yarborough, with Michihiko Oka and Masazumi Chaya, in Alvin Ailey's According to Eve *(1973). (Photo: Fred Fehl)*

Ruby Shang as Eve (stand-ing) and Eileen Cropley [as] an Elder, with Nicholas Gunn (below left) and Gr[eg] Reynolds (as Cain and Abel) in Paul Taylor's American Genesis, Act I[I,] *"West of Eden" (1973). (Photo: Kenn Duncan)*

Creation du Monde a "Ballet Nègre," as it was based on African cosmogony. His music contains elements of jazz — blues, for example — expressed in traditional, European forms, such as the fugue. It was first staged by the Swedish choreographer Jean Börlin in Paris in 1923, with primitivist sets by Fernand Léger.

Börlin used dancers walking on all fours and stilts to portray animals and birds, borrowing these devices from African native dance. At first there is a mass of bodies, as yet unformed, in the center of the dark stage. The three deities move around the bodies in magic incantation. The amorphous mass of bodies begins to move. First, a tree grows from its midst, then, in turn, an elephant, a turtle, a snake, and several monkeys are created. The stage grows lighter, a human leg appears, arms are raised, Man and Woman are born. They dance erotically while the rest of the dancers become demons. Gradually the frenzy subsides and the man and woman kiss each other. Milhaud's music inspired several choreographers, apart from those mentioned above, among them Agnes de Mille, who choreographed her *Black Ritual* to the score in 1940.

After the October Revolution in Russia in 1917, religious instruction in all schools was abolished, and there was an active antireligious movement, the *bezbozhniks* ("godless ones"), which spread atheist propaganda in the 1920s. Without judging the philosophical or social effect of such an attitude, surely the younger generation of Soviets grew up ignorant of the Bible, and this ignorance proved to be a barrier between them and understanding a large portion of Western culture, based as it is on Judeo-Christian ideas and symbols.

Nevertheless, in 1917, two Russian choreographers, Natalia Kasatkina and Vladimir Vasiliev, turned to the Biblical concept of Genesis as seen through the eyes of the French artist Jean Effel, and the Kirov Ballet of Leningrad premiered its *Creation of the World* to music by Andrei Petrov.

God was danced by Yuri Soloviev, who "created a character that is truly comic but does not lose its human spontaneity" (A. Dashicheva in *Sovetskaya kultura*, April 1971). Mikhail Baryshnikov (alternating with Vadim Guktaeyev) was Adam, Irina Kolpakova (alternating with Natalia Bolshkova) was Eve, and Valery Panov danced the Devil.

"The production had, apart from humor and fun, a rather lyrical tone," wrote Jana Hoskova (*Tanečni Listy*, Prague, November 1977). At first there is chaos, which angels try to tidy up while the Devil and his friends interfere. The world is an inflatable rubber ball, with which God and his cherubim play while the Devil and his brood disrupt their games.

Serge Lifar in the title role of his work, **David triomphant (1937),** *choreographed for the Paris Opera Ballet. (Photo: Lipnitzki, Dance Collection, Library and Museum of Performing Arts)*

LIPNITZKI
PARIS

The orb is not created by God, but is presented to Him by the sun. The powers of evil are unsuccessful and as a sort of revenge they plant the tree of the forbidden fruit with the well-known outcome of Fall and Expulsion.

Valery Panov, in his autobiography, *To Dance* (1978), thinks this was meant to be a chic Communist debunking of the Bible, as originated by two French communists. They depicted God creating light by igniting the sun with a cigarette lighter and creating the fish of the seas by throwing a sardine can into the waters. The Kirov Ballet version was, to him, "a far cruder version that smacked of the atheistic propaganda that bombarded us from our first day in kindergarten."

The choreographic signature of Adam is the well-known recumbent pose from Michelangelo's painting in the Sistine Chapel. God is more a chairman of the board than an autocrat, and Adam and Eve leave Eden by their own volition and find themselves in a hostile, earthly environment. The Devil follows them out of Eden. He has, by now, thrown off his guise as a merry *bon viveur* and appears in his true form as a demon. He destroys the world in one final atomic blast. The backdrop shows a torn Mona Lisa. A huge cloud of dust descends and menaces Adam and Eve. But a group of young people prop up behind them a semicircular structure — the beginning of new life — to the well-known chords from the last movement of Beethoven's Ninth, used as a quotation in Petrov's music. When de Valois recreated her *Création du Monde* for the Vic-Wells Ballet in 1935, she abandoned the Negro concept and the dancers appeared in "white face." Kenneth MacMillan again turned to Milhaud's *Création* in 1964.

Instead of the exotic-primitive idiom, MacMillan chose the landscape of children and their games to produce his pop creation, with set and costumes covered by ads and slogans by James Goddard. Teenagers, shod in kinky shoes, twist and shake, and God ("The Great Deity") wears a Union Jack on his shirt, because everyone knows God is an Englishman . . . .

The Biblical story has become a British joke.

God's first creation appears to be some sort of protoplasm which takes on the shapes of animals. The Serpent tempts Adam and Eve with an inflatable apple-balloon covered with advertisements. As they proceed to eat it, the apple shrinks. Adam and his girl turn their attention to each other and an erotic duet ensues. The Butcherboy, who appeared in the first part of the ballet, returns and carries the Deity off on the handlebars of his bicycle — a piece of symbolism which left several critics bewildered.

Standing (left to right), Sean Greene, Nora Reynolds, and Iris Pell in Bella Lewitzky's 1971 Pietas, a dance which depicts modern-day martyrdom. (Photo: Marion Valentine)

Frederick Ashton's *Walk to the Paradise Garden* (Royal Ballet, 1972) uses the Biblical image in a completely abstract manner, the one-act ballet showing the two ecstatic lovers finally meeting the Angel of Death, a sort of Paradise story in reverse.

In 1967 Roland Petit choreographed an Adam and Eve duet called *Paradis perdu,* to music by Marius Constant, for Margot Fonteyn and Rudolf Nureyev. At first there is a huge egg onstage, outlined in neon lights. There is a countdown of flashing lights, the egg bursts, and Adam is born. Alexander Bland described the ballet in an article in the London *Observer* as follows: "Then follows a series of solos and duets, Adam exploring his body, his first pain, as Eve is born, whom he regards at first without understanding and with suspicion, which later turns into harmony. The Serpent twists Eve into seduction and Adam into aggressive sexuality, ending in a theatrically breathtaking leap. Adam runs and jumps, head first, into the huge mouth of Eve painted on the backdrop."

why did cain kill his brother abel?

According to the Bible (Genesis 4:4), it was out of jealousy because "the Lord had respect unto Abel and to his offering, but unto Cain and his offering he had not respect."

In John Butler's *According to Eve* it was a case of sibling rivalry; jealousy over their mother's love and affection was the cause of aggression. A personal, psychological problem is substituted by the choreographer for the usual sociological explanation of the scholars, who see in the Cain-Abel story symbols of the ancient feud and conflict of interests between the nomad and shepherd, Abel, and the "tiller of the ground," the peasant Cain.

Kenneth MacMillan, in his version (Berlin 1968), starts like Butler with the Freudian notion of the sons competing for their mother's love and attention. However, MacMillan does not isolate the emotional problem from its social context, as Butler does, but puts it into the wider framework of an extended family unit. Eve is discovered entangled in a net of ribbons held by the chorus, perhaps representing society, "through which the principals weave their way in a series of complicated twisting and twining maneuvers, in which the characters tie themselves into different knots and break loose" (Alexander Bland, writing in *The Dancing Times*). "A sinister passage of drums [music by Polish composer Andrzej Panufnik] announces the beginning of a long encounter between the brothers, with the Snake intervening, which ends in a lengthy throttling. Cain is left filled with remorse"

*Francisco Ballet's
d McNaughton and
nis Marshall in* David
Goliath *(1975), jointly
eographed by Robert
h and Wayne Sleep.
to: James Armstrong)*

(*Ibid.*), rejected by the family (*i.e.*, society), which binds itself closely together again as Cain is left alone, dragging the body of his slain brother around the world forever.

Clement Crisp, writing in *The Financial Times*, London, interpreted the web in which Eve is entangled as a symbol of another Freudian concept, the Oedipus complex, the brothers' unconscious wish to sleep with their mother. According to John Percival's report (in *Dance and Dancers*), MacMillan was not at all interested in the story itself, but only in the images he was able to draw from it, "using the Biblical story . . . or really making up his own story and using the names just as a convenient way of telling you what to expect."

Sin Lieth at the Door, Israeli choreographer Moshe Efrati's Cain and Abel ballet, created for Batsheva in 1969, is done from "a male chauvinistic point of view" in Marcia Siegel's opinion. "The men, Efrati and Ehud Ben-David, dance up a storm in preparation for the disastrous denouement, except that instead of two contentious brothers they symbolize a creative misfit and a doomed conformist, with a well-meaning, but seductive Lady Demon (Rina Schoenfeld) getting the blame."

davids — combat and conflict

The story of David — small, vulnerable, refusing to don the armor he is unused to, the amateur defending his and his nation's freedom against the professional soldier, the aggressor Goliath, and winning against all odds — is a typical "ready made" Biblical story, begging to be choreographed.

The physical combat between uneven foes, and the theatrical opportunity of growing and shrinking before the very eyes of the spectator when the tale is done as a solo (as in the version of Marcel Marceau, who used a small screen from which on one side little David emerges, becoming the huge Goliath when coming out from the other side), has attracted many choreographers, among them Charles Weidman (1945), Robert North (London, 1975), and Dietmar Seyffert (East Berlin, in the early 1970s).

North expanded the *David and Goliath* duet to include crowd scenes in his all-male version with the London Contemporary Dance Theatre. "He and Wayne Sleep [alternating with Ross McKim] concentrate on an invented encounter before their battle, in which tiny Sleep somehow wins the confidence (maybe the love?) of the giant" (John Percival, in *Dance Magazine*, March 1976). Each protagonist has a solo to depict the character he is portraying. Goliath is "rather clumsy, presumably intended to show the character's brute stupidity," writes Percival.

Robert North and Wayne Sleep, of the London Contemporary Dance Theatre perform their own David and Goliath (1975). (Pho Anthony Crickmay)

King David inspired many more stage battles. While creators of modern dance tend to endow their Biblical battles with psychological insights, choreographed classical ballet usually remains on the epic, story-telling plane withholding comment, using the traditional Biblical images as they stand.

Such was the nature of Serge Lifar's *David triomphant* (Paris, 1937) to music by Debussy and Mussorgsky, with Lifar in the title role and Mia Slavenska as his wife Michal (King Saul's daughter, Melchola in the program).

David Lichine as David in Massine's work of the same name (in the early 1930s) "had simplicity and grandeur," according to Arnold Haskell. Max Terpis in Switzerland composed a scenario about the same subject and Keith Lester in London (1935), a ballet; both were in the broad epic manner. In London, Anton Dolin danced the eponymous role. Lifar tells in his autobiography that he was accused of being a Jew by the Nazis after the German occupation of France because of his Biblical ballets, *David triomphant* and *Song of Songs*. In fact, Lifar was neither Jewish nor interested in matters Jewish, but was simply after a good story which possessed qualities expressible in ballet terms.

Paul Sanasardo (in black) and Douglas Nielsen in Sanasardo's **Abandoned Prayer** *(1976). (Photo: Lor Greenfield)*

Shimon Braun and Moshe Efrati, of the Batsheva Dance Company, in Oshra Elkayam-Rumen's **David and Goliath**. *(Photo: Jaacov Agor)*

In José Limón's **There Is a Time**, *Limón dances with Pauline Koner in the scen "A Time to Embrace and a Time to Refrain from Embracing."*

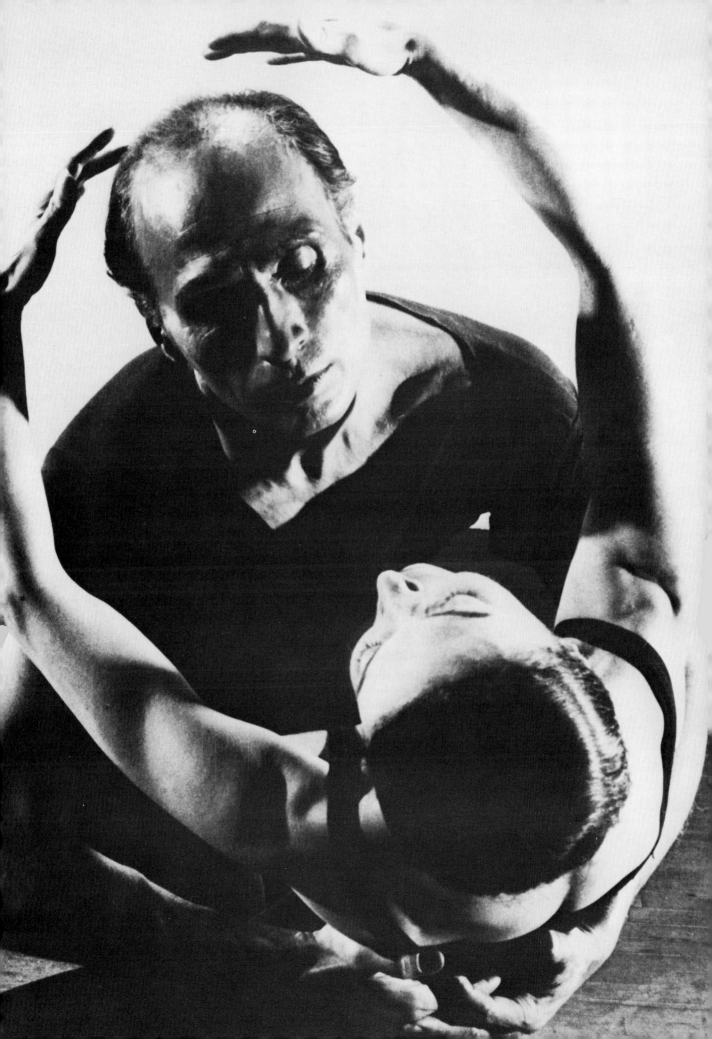

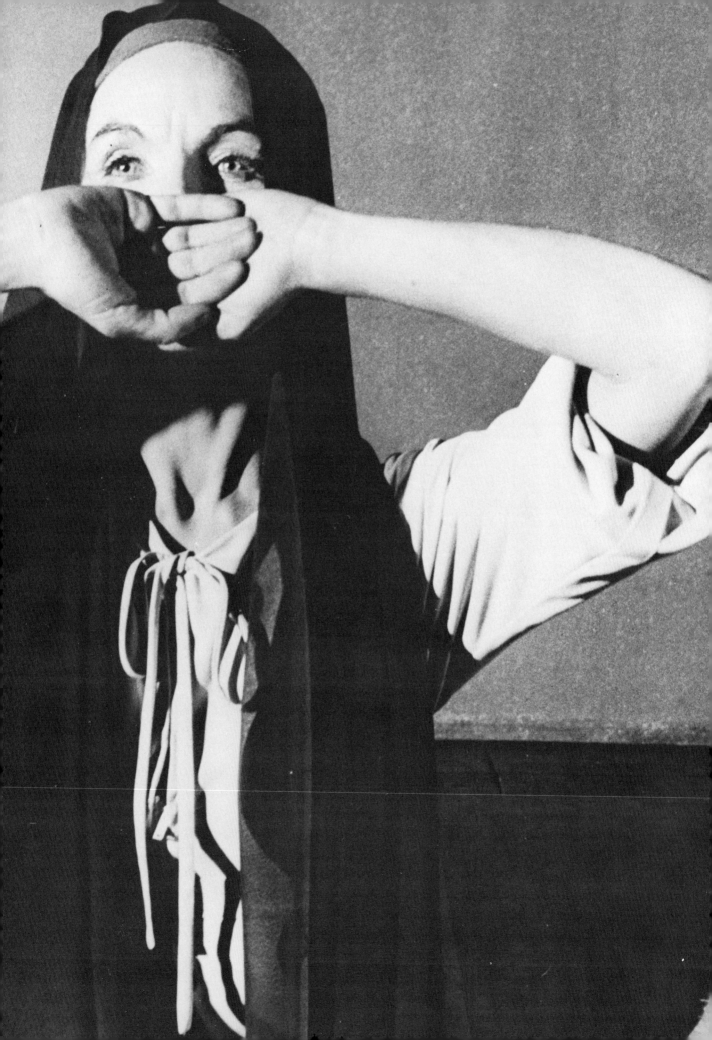

John Butler, a choreographer (and also a gentile) who often turns to Biblical themes for his work, states that he is not religious at all and that what fascinates him in these themes is their spellbinding plot, the profound drama, and forceful juxtaposition of dramatic and emotional opposites. A brilliant example of a completely abstract Biblical passage used for choreography is José Limón's *There is a Time* (based on Ecclesiastes 3). The text is based on the philosophical idea of life composed of contrasting complementary pairs of concepts and human activities, seemingly canceling each other, but in reality forming a dialectical progression of Hegelian or Marxist thesis and antithesis which together create the synthesis — the world as we know it. It is "one of the most completely realized large-scale works that Limón created," says Don McDonagh in *Complete Guide to Modern Dance*. "It is a presentation of a dozen episodes in the life of a community, both as a unit, in the beginning and in the end, and through individual numbers in selected variations." The circle is the formal expression of the community. The first solo (for a male dancer) deals with being born and dying. Four men and four women carry the dead one away and engage in sowing seed and reaping the harvest.

In the section "A Time to Kill," another man is slain by three others, and nursed by a woman in "A Time to Heal." Other sections are: "A Time to Break Down and a Time to Build Up," "A Time to Keep Silent and a Time to Speak," in which Limón casts the woman in the role of silence and the male dancer as the speaker; she keeps gesturing to calm her partner, to silence him while he stamps the floor and claps his hands, thus "dancing" his speech; "A Time to Mourn . . . a Time to Weep" is opposed to "A Time to Laugh . . . a Time to Dance"; and, finally, "A Time of Hate . . . A Time of War" is a solo for a woman, and yet another solo is given to a second dancer in "A Time of Love . . . A Time of Peace."

Lucas Hoving and Lavina Nielson in the scene "A Time to Speak and a Time to Keep Silent," from José Limón's **There Is a Time.**

The last part presents the circle again as each dancer executes an individual variation on the theme depicted in his or her previous solo. Limón, the master of content expressed perfectly through form in dance (for example, in *The Moor's Pavane)*, was attracted by Biblical subjects throughout his career. In 1945 he created *Eden Tree,* in 1947 *Song of Songs,* in 1950 *Exiles,* in 1954 *The Traitor,* in 1956 *There Is a Time,* and *Psalm* in 1967.

The Psalms, a book of poetry and prayers (and, according to some scholars, a book which contains many magical incantations which are used to this day to prevent the "evil eye" by Jewish-Yemenite and other rabbis) has provided a basis for several dance works, among these Ted Shawn's *Twenty-third Psalm* ("The Lord is my Shepherd, I shall not want . . . .") in 1921; Glen Tetley's *Tehilim* (the Hebrew word for *Psalms*) in 1966; James Truitte's *With Timbrel and Dance Praise His Name* (1973); Norman Walker's *Three Psalms* (1973); and Paul Sanasardo's *Hosanna* (1977). This list is far from complete.

biblical women

The Bible abounds in heroines. As modern dance was often dominated by women, their attention quite naturally turned to the Bible and the famous women it depicts. Despite the male-oriented ancient Oriental society which served as its matrix, the Bible devotes a lot of space to the female characters, who often excel in affairs of state and exert an influence even in the military sphere.

The Book of Judith was not included in the final Hebrew version of the Bible. Thus it belongs to the apocrypha, books included in the Septuagint and Vulgate translations of the Hebrew texts into Greek and Latin respectively but not written originally in Hebrew. Judith tells the story of a beautiful widow, Jael, who saved her native city of Bethulia when it was threatened by the Assyrian armies, first by inviting the general Sisera to her bed and later cutting off his head with his own sword. She appeared often in the Jesuit Biblical ballets, but also has a place in modern dance. Martha Graham first created a *Judith* solo for herself in 1950. In 1962 she turned again to the subject and created a large dance drama with a set by Dani Karavan and music by Mordecai Seter, both well-known Israeli artists who have collaborated with her often since.

There exist many versions of the story of Ruth, the faithful widow who follows her mother-in-law Naomi "home" to a land strange to her. The pastoral idyll of Ruth was used by Sara Levi-Tanai in her Inbal dance-drama of the same name (1961, set by Dani Karavan). Sophie Maslow (in 1964) and Yvonne

José Limón and Ruth Cu rier in Limón's Exiles *(1950).*

Georgi (Vienna, 1959) created *Ruth* solos, and Ruth was also one of the characters in Anna Sokolow's *Song of a Semite* (1944), which is a series of dances about Biblical heroines, including Miriam, sister of Moses, and others. Dore Hoyer, a German dancer, created her panorama, *Biblical Woman*, in 1942.

Esther, the Jewish queen of Persia who saved her nation from Haman's "final solution," is also frequently found in Jesuit ballet as well as modern repertoire, in works such as Ruth St. Denis's *Dancer at the Court of Ahasuerus* (1919), John Butler's *Esther* (1961), or Sokolow's *Esther the Queen* (1960).

Another popular heroine is Deborah. In a recent ballet by Moshe Efrati for Batsheva, in contrast to what most choreographers have made of the prophetess who led Barak's armies to victory, he used the subject as a lament for the dead soldiers soon after the Yom Kippur War. Efrati also choreographed a *Witch of Endor* (for Batsheva in 1970), another Biblical character often appearing in ballet.

Of course, there is also a long line of Delilahs, Jaels, and Marias who have populated the dance stage. The Bible has provided a vast galley of figures to identify with for the women who have created modern dance.

Martha Graham (standing), with Linda Hodes and Bertram Ross, in Graham's **Legend of Judith** *(1962). (Photo: Martha Swope)*

" . . . but Judith daughter of Merari disarmed him by the beauty of her face . . . ." (Judith 16:7)

Martha Graham and Bertram Ross in Graham's **Witch of Endor** *(1965). (Photo: Martha Swope)*

"And Ozias said to Judith 'My daughter, the blessing of God Most High is upon you, you are more than all other women on earth . . . (Judith 13:18)

the scandals of salome

In medieval illuminated manuscripts, she sometimes bends backwards until her palms touch the ground. On the windows of the cathedral in Bourges you see her doing a handstand, knees bent over her head. Hardly ten lines are devoted to her story in St. Mark's Gospel (6:14-29). Her name, Salome (*Shlomit* in Hebrew), does not appear in the Bible at all, and neither are her famous seven veils mentioned. Still, Salome, the dancer who is rewarded for her performance with the head of John the Baptist, Jokanaan, occurs persistently in literature, painting, and dancing through twenty centuries and is, perhaps, the most often used Biblical character on the modern dance stage.

The historical background in which the story originated is as follows: Herod, the tetrarch (Rome-appointed ruler) of Galilee, married his brother Philip's wife, Herodias. Jokanaan, the Baptist, publicly decried this, which was to him an adulterous and sinful liaison, calling Herodias a whore. Herod imprisoned Jokanaan.

Salome, whom some church authorities believe to have been Herod's own daughter, is asked to dance before the assembled court at Herod's birthday banquet. When she had done her dance "and pleased Herod . . . and sat with him, the king said unto the damsel, ask of me whatsoever thou wilt and I will give it thee . . . . And she went forth, and said unto her mother, What will I ask? And she said, The head of John the Baptist." The king was "exceeding sorry," but, because of his oath, sent for the executioners and John's head was brought in on a charger and given to "the damsel, and the damsel gave it to her mother."

Phyllis Curtin in the title role in a New York City Opera production of Richard Strauss's Salome. *(Photo: Fred Fehl)*

"And she, being before instructed of her mother, said, 'Give me here John Baptist's head in a charger.'" (Matthew 14:8)

The Canadian-born Maud Allan as she appeared in The Vision of Salome, *the work in which, in 1903, s made her debut as a dancer. (Photo: Dance Collection, Library and Museum of Performing Arts)*

In 1895 the Comédie Parisienne featured a pantomime *Salome* by Armand Sylvestre and Charles Henry Meltzer, in which the American dancer Loie Fuller portrayed Herodias's dancing daughter. Twelve years later, in 1907, she appeared in another Salome ballet, also in Paris. She used elaborate lighting apparatus and diaphanous veils for her dance, "entwined in strings of pearls taken from the coffers of Herodias." Fuller's dance of seduction was done in complete darkness, illuminated only by flashes of lightning. After the execution, she presented John's head on a charger in a triumphal dance and finale. In the "Dance of Fear," Salome ran all over the stage "to flee panic-stricken from the sight of the severed head persistently following her with martyred eyes."

Diaghliev, who saw the performance, was attracted by this rather sensational treatment and five years later his company performed a Salome ballet in Paris and London with choreography by Boris Romanoff, the eponymous character being danced by Tamara Karsavina.

Oscar Wilde's play *Salome*, first published in French in 1893, was a much more sophisticated treatment of the Biblical story. Wilde builds the tension by adding Salome's passion for Jokanaan — for his wild eyes and red lips — to the traditional revenge motive of her mother. Salome is now not a "good girl obeying her mother," but a lascivious creature, torn between her attraction for and repulsion of the fanatic ascetic incarcerated in the palace dungeon. Thus, another sensual layer is added to the already charged atmosphere of the original story. "It is thy mouth that I desire, Jokanaan. Thy mouth is like a band of scarlet on a

As Salome, Maude Allan toured Europe in 1907, performing her "scandalous" Dance of Salome, a two-part work consisting of "The Dance of Salome" and "The Vision of Salome." (Photos: Dance Collection, Library and Museum of Performing Arts)

"And his head was brought in a charger, and given to the damsel: and she brought it to her mother." (Matthew 14:11)

Lucas Cranach's painting, Salome. (Photo: The Bettmann Archive)

tower of ivory," Salome exclaims in Wilde's play.

The lascivious, colorfully decadent play aroused the wrath of censors and upright burghers and also the imagination of another American dancer, Maude Allan. In 1907 she performed her *Dance of Salome* all over Europe. In Munich "The 'Censur' [*sic*] had given its blessing, and all seemed satisfied, when suddenly a *verbot* [ban] from the Bavarian Government was issued against me," she writes in her autobiography. Articles pro and con were published in the newspapers, but the powers-that-be would not yield, and the performance was finally held as a "subscription concert." Later, during World War I, Allan again got into trouble and litigation because of her Salome. Her dance consisted of two parts: "The Dance of Salome" and "The Vision of Salome."

"I want you to see, as I can, in imagination," she writes in her autobiography, "the sombre splendour of those pillared halls, princess Salome, hardly more than a child . . . . Hardly has she become reconciled to calling Herod Antipas by the dearer name of 'Father,' when she witnessed one never-to-be-forgotten day, the fury of her mother," when she is summoned to dance before the assembled court. "The rude, plaintive cadences of the native musicians restore [her] faltering confidence . . . and she weaves her most ingenious witcheries of dance."

Finally, "she stands panting, aghast, her hands pressed to her young breasts; she raises them, and, bowing her head to meet them, sees upon her naked flesh, upon the hands that seek her smarting eyes, the purple, sticky stain that she has not been able to avoid," the blood of the dead man. She stands petrified and the whole scene comes back to her, in the "Vision of Salome."

As "in a dream [she] descends the marble steps. . . . slowly, to the strains of the distant music, reminiscently she raises her willowy arms. A voice whispers, 'your duty.' Does not the child owe obedience to its mother?" In the mad whirl of childish joy she is drawn again to dance. Soon, exhaustion breaks the spell. Salome, princess of Galilee, lies prone on the cold grey marble. Now, instead of wanting to conquer, she wishes to be conquered, craving the spiritual guidance of the man whose wrath is before her; but it remains silent. She begs and prays for mercy of the stern head — alas without response! Salome flees in despair, "her soul rejoicing towards Salvation . . . . A sudden grief overmasters her, and the fair princess, bereft of her pride, her childish gaiety and her womanly desire, falls, her hands grasping high above her for her lost redemption, a quivering huddled mass. It is the atonement for her mother's awful sin!"

English dance-mime artist Lindsay Kemp's bizarre adaptation of Oscar Wilde's Salome featured Kemp in the title role and David Haughton as John the Baptist. (Photo: Herb Migdoll)

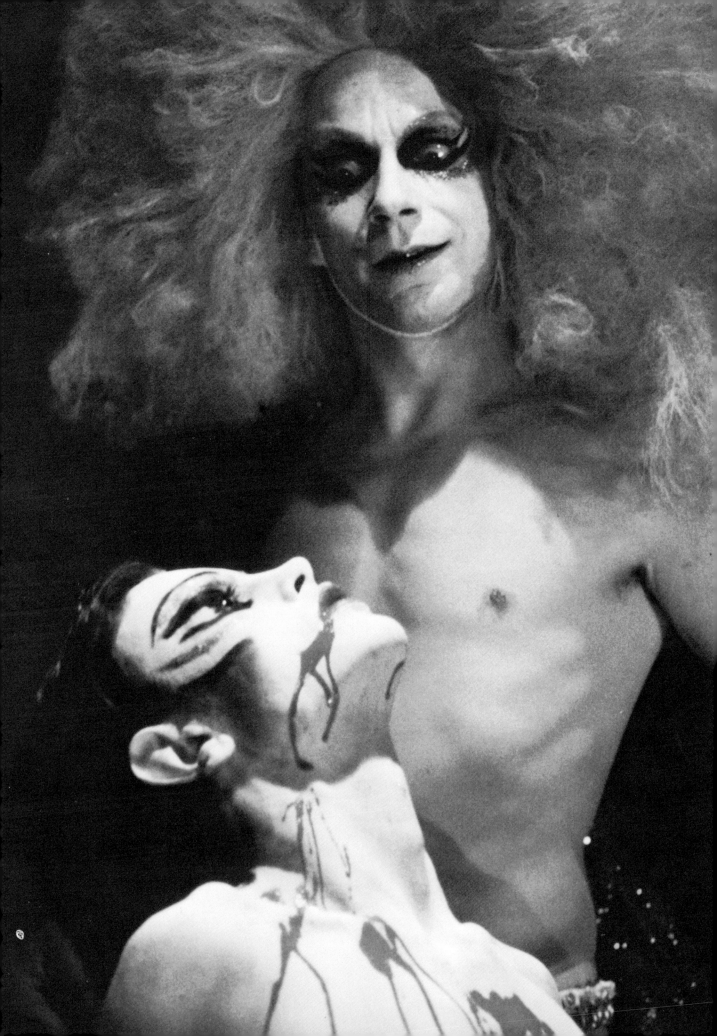

Salome, *a depiction by* **Jules LeFebvre.** *(The* **Bettmann Archive)**

All these lofty sentiments did not save Maude Allan from scandal. Dressed only in many rows of large pearls, the sensuous aspect of her dance dominated the scene. In 1918 she filed a libel suit against one Noel Pemberton Billing, British M.P., crank and journalist, who had accused her of being a lesbian and a sadist when she was about to appear in Wilde's *Salome* in London. He wrote an article about her dancing in his paper, *The Vigilante,* titled "The Cult of the Clitoris." After a somewhat farcical, six-day trial, the judge ruled in the defendant's favor.

Salome and her lascivious dance, her morbid love-hate for the imprisoned prophet and ascetic, and the whole torpid atmosphere of Herod's court kept many artists' minds churning out material not only in dance. Gustave Flaubert wrote a novel, Heinrich Heine a poem, Stéphane Mallarmé a *Herodiade,* which was later to become the inspiration for Martha Graham's duet of that title.

Richard Strauss composed an opera, *Salome,* first staged in Dresden in 1905, in which Salome's dance is of crucial importance, and it was regarded by contemporaries as a "musical perversity." According to the composer himself, he saw it performed only once to perfection, when Ruth Sorel (Abramowitch) danced Salome in Warsaw in 1933 at a dance contest as a solo and out of the context of the opera (choreography by Alexander Gorsky). Three years after Sorel, Mia Slavenska, the Yugoslav ballerina, then only eighteen years old, danced a very different Salome at the International Dance Festival in Berlin. "She did not dance Salome, the seductress, but sought to portray a symbolic dramatic figure who persists in the conflict between 'her abominable inheritance of crime and vice' and 'the immortal law of life,' " to the music of Alexander Glazounov. So wrote Arthur Michel in 1946 in *In Dance.*

Slavenska's mentor and teacher, Gertrud Kraus, created her *Salome* in Tel Aviv in 1946. Her solo linked the New Testament story to Old Testament material, namely the Song of Songs, and did not contain the traditional "striptease" element of the seven veils, which in any case is not of Biblical origin but a medieval embellishment. For her, Salome was another opportunity to return to the theme of love which leads inevitably into death, of life which embraces death and therefore must die, an idea often found in this remarkable Expressionistic dancer's work.

An endless procession of Salomes has danced across the stages of the world since the beginning of the twentieth century. Alexander Gorsky's in 1921 and Kassian Goleizovsky's in 1924, in Russia; Ruth St. Denis's in 1931; Serge Lifar's in 1946; Birgit

Loie Fuller in **Salome** *costume, 1895. (Photo: Bosch, Dance Collectio Library and Museum of Performing Arts)*

Cullberg's in Sweden in 1964; Joseph Lazzini's in 1968; Peter Durrel's in London, 1970; Maurice Béjart's in Paris in 1970; and many others. A rather special *Salome* was staged in London by Lindsay Kemp, in an all-male camp version. "A cape of green plumage, half exotic bird and half Kew Gardens, which is whipped away to reveal a skin-tight costume fetchingly decorated with spiral bands of colour and a few sequins" is Geoff Brown's description of Kemp's *Salome (Plays & Players*, March 1977). In this production, Queen Herodias sports a bald pate, bulbous breasts and black lips. The arena stage engulfed the audience in a smell of burning incense and the sound of percussion instruments with snatches of Wagner.

In 1909, when Ida Rubinstein was to be Diaghilev's Salome, her costume was designed by Bakst, but was suppressed by the censor as too daring. Nobody was shocked by Kemp's bare bodies in 1977.

But the choreographer who returned again and again to Salome, and made it one of his masterpieces, was Lester Horton. No less than six Salomes were danced by Horton's company between 1931, which saw the first one, and 1950 when *The Face of Violence* became his final version. *Salome* of the year 1932 was Horton's first choreodrama. The costumes were theatrically bold, combining ancient silhouettes with a modern line — Salome's skirt somewhat in the manner of Minoan art; Jokanaan in a robe, one shoulder bare, the other arm in a wide sleeve; Herodias in a tall, Persian headdress, her "evening gown" emphasizing the breasts, while Salome's flesh-colored dress had the nipples and navel painted on. The music accompanying Horton's first *Salome* was by Constance Boynton and had an Oriental flavor. Horton himself danced the role of Herod, and Brahm van den Berg that of Jokanaan. The *Los Angeles Times* critic described Horton in the role as "imbued with dramatic strength, never deviating from a drunken, half-mad character sunk in sensuality." For Horton, Salome was a "study in the pathology of decadence" (program note from 1948); in his frequent remakings of the piece in 1945 and later, the ancient legend became a modern comment on violence. By the time Bella Lewitzky danced the role, the Salome costume had become a simple, long dress. Still, the sensuality of Horton's interpretation shocked the *Los Angeles Herald-Express*: "*Salome* is a remarkably theatrical piece that goes just as far as possible on the public stage without calling in the police." One wonders whether today, when taboo after taboo has been demolished in modern theater, the shock would be

Karen Kuertz of the Cincinnati Ballet Company in James Truitte's Face of Violence (Salome), *adapted from Lester Horton's original of the same title. (Photo: Sandy Underwood)*

as potent as it was then. But Horton was not interested in just shocking his spectators. The importance of his Biblical choreodrama lies in its theatricality and satire. Revived in 1973 by Carmen de Lavallade and James Truitte in Cincinnati, *Dance Magazine's* reviewer found it "a violent, poignant, beautiful piece." Perhaps in today's world of terrorism, hijacking, and kidnappings, even more so than in the 1940s, this pathology of decadence carries a relevant message. The *Dance Magazine* reviewer describes the dance thus:

Amidst ramps and platforms Salome advances with diagonal lunges, twirling a fan above her head. She slithers over to a Guard (Wayne Maurer), seduces him, and wins her request for the release of John the Baptist (Michael Bradshaw). Writhing her body against this newest victim, it is obvious that she is a wanton woman bent on an evil mission. She grows progressively stronger and more vicious, vanquishing both men. Horton's percussive score, "glove-fit" to the production, sustains the drama and tension. The second scene introduces Herodias, the doddering Herod, and his Eunuch (who doubles as the Greek chorus). Their decadence is apparent both in dress and activity. Salome performs her Dance of the Seven Veils, but the most potent imagery is when she dances with the gory, bloodstained cloth that covered John the Baptist's head. Clutched between her teeth, pressed against her body, the material assumes its own sinister character. And in the end, Herod uses it to strangle her.

A nineteenth-century engraving: **Salome Dancing Before King Herod.** *(The Bettmann Archive)*

"But when Herod's birthday was kept, the daughter of Herodias danced before them, and pleased Herod." *(Matthew 14:6)*

Hildegard Behrens in the title role of the Richard Strauss opera Salome, *in a performance at the Salzburg Summer Festival in 1977.*

This description refers to Horton's final version as revived twenty years after its premiere. The accompaniment was by Horton himself and was entirely played on percussion instruments which he had collected for many years. His score was judged by Aaron Copland to be the best percussion piece for dance he had ever heard. "It was played live for the first performances. As the dancers sat behind a scrim at the rear of the stage, the human voice was interwoven with the myriad sounds." Horton himself wrote about his 1948 version: "[The earlier versions] were to a considerable extent dependent on the Wildean concept. Which is to say a relatively superficial one from the standpoint of inner motivations, for Wilde was fascinated by the surface terror, the superficial shock, the poetry of words and images. . . . This time I started to examine the motives more thoroughly. I turned, I think, to Freud." Larry Warren in his book about Horton does not quite accept this opinion, though he says, "Horton may have seen as Freudian his development of the character of Herodias," and "the range of Salome's perversity, too, was broadened in this version as hints of onanism, foot-fetishism and incest appeared [to be developed in later versions], but the work remained essentially a powerful theatrical statement and not one that is psychologically revealing to any great extent."

Perhaps the truly subtle psychological treatment of the Salome theme, and at the same time the most abstract one, in which the horror is just hinted at and no external action or violence occurs, is to be found in Martha Graham's *Herodiade* (1944).

With music by Paul Hindemith and a set by Isamu Noguchi, Graham created a duet for two dancers, A Woman (Herodias) and Her Attendant. At first, the work was titled *Mirror Before Me*, which points to Graham's source of inspiration, namely the French Symbolist poet Stéphane Mallarmé's poem of the same name. In the poem Herodias, Narcissus-like, gazes at herself in "the cold water" of her mirror and asks, "Nurse, am I beautiful?" She forbids the nurse ever to mention Jokanaan, him in whom "destiny guards our secrets," and she says, "I love virginity's horror," but when alone, confesses, "I await a thing unknown."

In the oldest versions of the Salome legend it was always Herodias, the adulterous queen, the heroine's mother, who pushed the young princess to demand John the Baptist's head, and it was the older woman who was the real villain. In Maude Allan's *Salome,* she even tried to exonerate herself by stressing her duty to her mother and the obedience she owes her. Thus, Salome's sensuality is, in a way, a mirror-image of her mother's

The Ruth St. Denis Salo[me] was given its premiere by the Denishawn Dancers [in] Richmond, Virginia, in February 1931. In this photo, taken at Jacob's Pillow in 1950, St. Deni[s] poses in her Beardsley-inspired Salome costum[e] (Photo: John Lindquist, Dance Collection, Librar[y] and Museum of Performi[ng] Arts)

promiscuity. So, perhaps, Herodias is really gazing at her daughter's face, so similar to her own, in the mirror.

In Graham's *Herodiade* we see the tragedy reflected in the figure of the mother; the whole dance, a miniature of exquisite clarity and jewel-like brilliance, is a preparation, a ritual preceding the fateful event itself, which we never witness, but feel as a premonition.

Herodias is seated at a stylized dressing table, the stool and the table forming one piece of sculpture. In the program notes we read: "The scene is an antechamber where a woman waits with her attendant. She does not know for what she waits; she does not know what she may be required to do or endure, and the time of waiting becomes a time of preparation. A mirror provokes an anguish of scrutiny; images of the past, fragments of dreams float to its cold surface, add to the woman's agony of consciousness. With self-knowledge comes acceptance of her mysterious destiny; this is the moment when waiting ends. Solemnly the attendant prepares her. As she advances to meet the unknown, the curtain falls."

At first Herodias, frightened, runs around, kneels on the stool attached to the mirror-table. Repeatedly,

Martha Graham in the title role of her Herodiade *(1944), an interpretation of events in the life of Salome's mother. (Photo: Arnold Eagle)*

Seen in Martha Graham' Point of Crossing (given premiere in December 1975 and based on Graham's 1974 work, Jacob's Dream) are Yuri Kimura and Ross Parkes (Photo: Martha Swope)

she goes down on her knees as in prayer, her attendant kneeling next to her. The attendant attempts to lift her without actually touching her. Herodias rises and dances. Her eyes are fixed on the mirror. Finally she turns and starts to exit, as the lights fade. What remains of the story are the inner stirrings of a soul in torment. The plot itself is reduced, or rather distilled, into the emotional quintessence of the situation.

This is far removed from the sensational, exotic dance of the seven veils, the strings of pearls. The striptease of the body in so many interpretations becomes a baring of the soul in Graham. And yet, all the tension and dramatic fascination of the Biblical story is, somehow, still there. A remarkable feat of abstraction.

Flemming Flindt staged his version of *Salome* in the old Circus Building in Copenhagen in the fall of 1978, using music by Peter Maxwell Davies and set and costumes by Bernard Dayde. Flindt's *Salome* is a "political" Biblical work which shows the Jewish farmers as being oppressed by the Roman soldiers and Herod as a Roman puppet. The struggle for power is depicted through a scene in which Herod, Philip Herodias, and Herod's wife, Aretas (later poisoned by Herodias), fight for the crown. Herod has imprisoned, but does not dare to execute, John the Baptist, whom Salome visits in jail. Salome (Vivi Flindt) falls in love with the Baptist and, when he is brought in to amuse the guests at Herod's feast, Salome dances for Herod to save John from humiliation. But she does not, as tradition has it, titillate him by shedding the seven veils one by one; instead, she defiantly pulls off all her clothes and dances naked. Herod, unable to overcome his lust, seizes her and makes love to her in front of the whole court.

After the execution of the Baptist, "in an apotheosis, she and John, both dressed in white, dance joyously together in the river of redemption" (John Percival in *Dance and Dancers*, January 1979.)

Flindt, who danced the role of Herod himself, is first of all a man of the theater. His ballets are always powerful shows. So, most critics agree, is his *Salome*. His idea of putting the story into a wider framework of history is new, but making Herodias (danced by Lizzie Rode) the sole villain connects his version to the older works based on the story of Salome.

Flemming Flindt, as Herod, and Vivi Flindt in the title role of Salome, his new work for the Royal Danish Ballet. The piece became the artistic event most discussed in Copenhagen, both in the ballet world and outside. (Photo: Claus Ørsted)

joseph — the victory of innocence

Joseph, the son of the patriarch Jacob, is sold by his brothers into slavery. He is bought by Potiphar, Pharaoh's captain of the guard, and, in due course, becomes the overseer of the captain's household. "His master's wife cast her eyes upon Joseph; and she said, 'lie with me,' according to Genesis 39:7. "And it came to pass, as she spake to Joseph day by day, that he harkened not to her, to lie with her. . . . Joseph went into the house to do his business; and there were none of the men of the house there within. And she caught him by his garment in her hand, saying, 'Lie with me,' and he left his garment in her hand, and fled, and got him out."

Joseph's garment in Potiphar's hand becomes her evidence against him and her tool of revenge. She accuses him of attacking her, and Joseph is thrown into a dungeon.

In 1912 the Viennese author and poet Hugo von Hofmannsthal saw Diaghilev's ballet company and was so impressed that he wrote a letter to composer Richard Strauss in which he suggested writing a ballet for the Ballets Russes. The project finally took shape with the help of Harry Graf Kessler, a friend of Hofmannsthal, and became the libretto of *Joseph in Egypt* (later titled *Josephslegende*, as the term "legend" seemed more appropriate to a mimed drama in which one of the central figures, that of Potiphar's Wife, was not a dancing role at all). In another letter to Strauss, Hofmannsthal writes: " . . . I made a short ballet . . . the episode of Potiphar's Wife; [the role of] the youthful Joseph naturally for Nijinsky, the most extraordinary man the contemporary stage possesses. . . . What I deem good in this proposal, if I am not erring, is twofold: the idea to clothe the Biblical subject in costumes in the style and spirit of Paolo Veronese [a Venetian painter, 1528 - 1588, whose clean colors anticipated eighteenth-century style] and emphasizing the dramatic antithesis of the two main characters, who, finally, polarly opposed, go, one to the bright heavens above and the other to sudden death and damnation."

At first the work did not progress easily, as Strauss found it difficult to choose a proper "religious" musical theme for the virtuous Joseph. His first attempts were severely criticized by Hofmannsthal. Strauss promised to try again to come up with something more appropriate. In another letter Hofmannsthal points out that Joseph does not require a religious theme at all, but rather something pure, innocent, as he is "a shepherd, a gifted son of a mountain-dwelling nation . . . and his search for God [is expressed with] wide leaps."

Hofmannsthal had long talks with Diaghilev, who

Leonide Massine in the title role of The Legend of Joseph, *choreographed by Michel Fokine in 1914 for Diaghilev's Ballets Russes (Photo: Courtesy of the Stravinsky-Diaghilev Foundation)*

decided to appoint Fokine to choreograph the ballet and to cast Nijinsky in the title role. But when the time for the premiere arrived (Paris, May 14, 1914), Nijinsky was no longer a member of the company and the young and as yet unknown Leonide Massine danced the part of Joseph. The singer Maria Kusnetzova created the role of Potiphar's Wife, a bit of casting which became traditional. The set — green and golden with convoluted columns and ramps after the manner of Veronese — was by the Spanish painter José Maria Sert, and the costumes were designed by Bakst. But Diaghilev did not like Joseph's costume and this was changed at the last minute to a simple goatskin tunic, which left the dancer's thighs bare and prompted the Parisian public to dub the ballet "Les Jambes de Joseph." The critical reception was only lukewarm. A lot of spectacle, too little dancing, was the general verdict.

In the librettist's own words, the scene is " . . . a sumptuous chamber which mirrors the decadent, opulent, scintillating bloom of swamp plants and unbridled consumption." Perhaps this orchidlike richness also belonged in a way to the era about to come to an end a few weeks after the premiere with the shots fired by Gavrilo Princip in Sarajevo.

Potiphar and his wife preside over a banquet. An erotic dance by female slaves is led by Potiphar's favorite, the court dancer Sulamith (curiously enough, this is the name of the main character in the Biblical book, Song of Songs). A boxing match and a dance by whip-wielding male black slaves follow. Potiphar's wife remains motionless throughout all these entertainments. Joseph is brought in, in a golden net borne by two slave traders. His solo, full of innocence and trust in God, arouses the interest of Potiphar's wife. Joseph is bought. The banquet ends and as the court leaves, Joseph is shown his quarters by the major-domo. He lies down and falls asleep. An angel appears to him in his dream. Potiphar's wife returns and stands looking upon the sleeping Joseph. She kisses him and he opens his eyes. She tries to seduce him by a sensual dance, but he modestly turns his gaze away from her. His rejection turns her lust into hatred. She tries to strangle him, but he succeeds in freeing himself. Servants come running in, he is thrown into chains, and she tears his mantle off him. Torturers bring forth a brazier with burning coals and proceed to heat instruments of torture in the flames. A miracle occurs — the angel appears and delivers Joseph from his chains and leads him away. Potiphar's wife commits suicide by strangling herself with her strings of pearls.

This page and following: Judith Jamison and Kevin Haigen, as Joseph and Potiphar's wife, in John Neumeier's **The Legend of Joseph** *(1977), created for the Vienna State Opera Ballet. (Photos: right, Palffy; following pages, Benn)*

"And it came to pass . . . that his master's wife cast her eyes upon Joseph; and she said, 'Lie with me.' But he refused . . . . And she caught him by his garment, saying, 'Lie with me': and he left his garment in her hand, and fled . . . . " *(Genesis 39:1-23)*

Massine, still in his teens, accustomed to the strict discipline of line and structure of classical Russian ballet, was perplexed by Fokine's free-flowing movement in the crowd scenes. His first solo, which expressed the boy's bewilderment when facing the strange grandeur of the Egyptian court, was very modern in concept, well outside the traditional ballet steps he was used to. It was composed of great leaps, alternating with running steps and kneeling poses. Massine's second solo, however, was more conventional and involved less mime, and he felt more at ease in it.

The Legend of Joseph has been revived often in various forms and everchanging choreography. In 1921 Heinrich Kröller produced it in Munich and Berlin, and a year later, in Vienna, the city where it was conceived. George Balanchine created his *Joseph* in Copenhagen in 1931, and other productions were by Aurel von Milloss, Margarethe Wallmann, Pia and Pino Mlakar, Antony Tudor, and many others.

Kassian Goleizovsky, one of the most original and innovative of Soviet choreographers, turned his attention to the story of Joseph in 1925. A year earlier he had created his *Salome*, and again a Biblical subject caught his imagination. He and his colleague Fyodor Lopokov were the leaders of the avant-garde in Russian ballet. Both believed that the art of ballet had to find new subject matter to be expressed in novel forms if it wished to remain in touch with the changing times. They both felt that after the October Revolution there had to be a fundamental change in the traditional ballet, as all values and indeed the whole social order in Russia had radically changed. Lopokov believed that this change should be attempted while preserving the fundamental forms of classicism, while Goleizovsky argued that the new ballet would have to invent its own, new, movement vocabulary. Soviet theater was brimming with experiment, and Goleizovsky used the new ideas of Constructivism to great advantage in his *Joseph the Beautiful,* which was premiered at the Experimental Stage of the Bolshoi in Moscow.

The music was by the Ukrainian composer Sergei Vassilenko, the set by B. Erdman. Goleizovsky and his designer discarded the traditional painted backdrops and flats and built a three-dimensional set which consisted of rostrums, platforms and connecting bridges, in true Constructivist style. The costumes, also by Erdman, were scant, leaving the dancers' bodies seminude. Even the dancers' skins were painted and made-up according to a color scheme devised by the designer: orange for the

Jews, red for Egyptians. "Joseph was a lemon-yellow youth with feminine features. . . . Potiphar's wife was white as milk. She appeared upon the stage with only narrow silver strips over bust and hips. Her bobbed black hair was parted in the middle by a string of diamonds." This is how Zachary L. McLove describes the ballet, banned by the Moscow Soviet as "immoral," in the *New York Times Magazine* of November 15, 1925. Erdman's costumes show strips of material wound around the dancers' arms and legs, reminding one of the ritual leather ribbons of the phylacteries, worn on the left arm and forehead by Jewish men during prayer. All those innovations and breaches of traditional "laws" created a scandal and outraged the conservative critics.

The ballet was divided into two acts. In the first one, the platforms and connecting planks created a flowing landscape, the hills of Canaan, Joseph's homeland. The idyllic atmosphere of the shepherd's youth was expressed in the accompanying soft flute music, and Joseph himself danced playing the ancient reed instrument, the shawm. The choreography established the protagonist's character as a dreamer, a sensitive, vulnerable, artistic soul.

For the second act the platforms were turned around and rearranged to form a broad, majestic staircase. Instead of the broken lines of the hilly landscape, where the dancers performed on top and beneath the set units, a symmetrical, courtly structure, flanked by columns, represented the imperial Egyptian palace of Potiphar.

The pyramid was used in the set and in the choreography to symbolize power. To the strains of a festive march, the court entered. On a royal palanquin, Potiphar's spouse was brought in, followed by the ruler himself. Groups of halberd bearers formed the flanks of the procession, as the stage lights progressively revealed a gigantic triangle of people — the symbolic pyramid. At its apex the ruler stood like a bird of prey, in a high headdress, his arms spread apart.

Into this symmetrical, formal structure Joseph is cast, brought for sale by slave traders. He scorns the approaches of Potiphar's wife and finally throws himself into the abyss from the top of the structure. In the final dance, all the courtiers and servants pay him homage and, as they move, the huge pyramid which they formed crumbles. They mix and mingle as if the rigid laws that bound them had disintegrated, the whole oppressive structure of tyranny broken.

While for Diaghilev *Josephslegende* was another exotic ballet, for Hofmannsthal and Kessler it represented first of all the triumph of innocence over depravity. Goleizovsky's *Joseph the Beautiful* was, in a way, an "anarchistic" ballet. His true protagonist was not the individual but society as a whole: a free, individualistic peasant society juxtaposed to a rigid, cruel, autocratic rule.

The year 1925 marked, in fact, the end of the experimental era of Soviet art which had begun after the Revolution. By then, Stalin's cultural commissars had taken over from the enlightened, liberal Minister of Culture Lunacharsky, and all experiments had to cease. Russian ballet was back in the traditional compound, where it had flourished under the czars.

When John Neumeier turned to *Josephslegende* in 1977, he found the sixty-year-old libretto not quite to his liking. He also thought the ballet music composed by Richard Strauss "too grand and pompous for the simple story" (program notes). Instead he used a "Symphonic Fragment" prepared by the composer from his *Joseph* material for concert hall performance.

Neumeier says in the program notes to his production at the Vienna State Opera: "This composition sketches in a clear line all I find interesting in the *Joseph* theme, namely the Biblical idea of a chosen one, who is suspended, swinging between two worlds, the human (earthly) and the metaphysical one, between which he has to choose."

Neumeier was astonished at the compact way the Bible tells the story. He realized that one has to see the Potiphar episode in the context of Joseph's destiny as savior of his nation. The *deus ex machina* appearance of the delivering angel, clad in gold, at the end of the Hofmannsthal libretto, seemed to him insufficient, even "a bit ridiculous." The original version included little dancing but a lot of mime (one of the reasons it originally was called a *mystery* or a *legend* rather than a *ballet*).

Neumeier states: "One being seduced but remaining steadfast is not sufficient material for a whole work. I deemed it more important to show the process Joseph has to go through before he is ready to fulfill his task; he 'learns to fly' only at the very end of the story. In my version only then he embarks on his mission."

Therefore, he expanded the Angel's role. Joseph dreams about the Angel even before he is sold into Egypt, in a sort of prologue. At Potiphar's court a feast is in progress, but Potiphar's wife refuses to take part in the festivities. To entertain the guests, a wrestling match is arranged, but the victor is in his turn vanquished by a mysterious, beautiful stranger, the Angel. (One is reminded of the Angel of God wrestling with Jacob.) Joseph is brought in and sold

Judith Jamison and Kevin Haigen in John Neumeier's **The Legend of Joseph.** *(Photo: Benn)*

"And it came to pass, as she spake to Joseph day by day, that he hearkened not unto her, to lie by her, or to be with her."
(Genesis 39:10)

to be a slave of Potiphar's court. He dances and his mistress is deeply impressed. The guests leave and Joseph, alone, falls asleep. The Angel appears to him in his dream. Potiphar's wife returns to where Joseph lies sleeping but is surprised by her husband, who orders Joseph tortured. Potiphar's wife strikes Joseph, but something deep inside her makes her take his side against her husband. The Angel comes and leads Joseph away, and Potiphar's wife remains alone.

Brilliant casting — Judith Jamison in the role of Potiphar's wife (discarding the traditional casting of a nondancer in this part), the young American dancer Kevin Haigen in the title role, and Karl Musil as the Angel — and the inventive choreography turned the flawed masterpiece into a real gem half a century after its first performance. A Biblical extravaganza became a modern ballet, which, in a way, succeeded in recovering the values of the ancient original.

a philosophical masque: job

The Book of Job is one of the works which the compilers of the Old Testament found difficult to include in their selection. The sages deemed the story blasphemous. Job questions heaven and he voices his doubts of God's eternal justice, imputing to him a capacity for immoral or amoral decisions. The story of Job seemed heretic: that a righteous man should come to grief, become a victim of and a

Ted Shawn and the Denishawn Dancers in Jo (Photo: Dance Collectio Library and Museum of Performing Arts)

"And the Lord said unto Satan, 'Has thou considered my servant Job, that there is none like hi in the earth, a perfect an an upright man, one that feareth God, and escheweth evil?'" (Job 1:

Paul Haakon (kneeling) i Ted Shawn's Job, A Masc for Dancing, first perform at Lewisohn Stadium, New York, in 1931. (Pho Dance Collection, Librar and Museum of Performi Arts)

Ted Shawn and the Denishawn Dancers in Shawn's Job, A Masque for Dancing, after drawings by William Blake. (Photo: Dance Collection, Library and Museum of Performing Arts)

pawn in a contest between God and Satan, lose his children and his livelihood, his body stricken with boils in order to test his steadfastness. Only after a "new, revised ending" was added to the material (Elihu's speech) did the book become acceptable and pass the censor's scrutiny.

In many respects Job's skepticism is very modern. His rebellion against the highest authority could be voiced by those who had to endure the tortures of Nazi concentration camps, A-bombs, gas attacks and all the other forms of our century's organized horrors. Job's outcry is the eternal *Why?* of man's suffering.

Ted Shawn in his **The Twenty-third Psalm** *(1915). (Photo: Edward Henry Weston, Dance Collection, Library and Museum of Performing Arts)*

"Yea, though I walk through the valley of the shadow of death, I will fear no evil, for thou art with me; thy rod and thy staff they comfort me . . . ." (Psalms 23:4)

Ted Shawn as he appeared in his **Dance of David** *(1919-20). (Photo: Denishawn Collection, Dance Collection, Library and Museum of Performing Arts)*

"I will praise thee, O Lord, among the people: and I will sing praises unto thee among the nations. For thy mercy is great above the heavens: and thy truth reacheth unto the clouds. (Psalms 108:3-4)

Members of the Sadler's
Wells Ballet in two scenes
from the 1948 revival of
Dame Ninette de Valois's
Job (1931), with Robert
Helpmann as Satan (on
throne). Like Ted Shawn's
Job, A Masque for Dancing,
de Valois's work also used
the music of Ralph
Vaughan Williams and the
drawings of William Blake
as inspiration. (Photo:
Dance Collection, Library
and Museum of Performing
Arts)

*"Again there was a day
when the sons of God came
to present themselves
before the Lord, and Satan
came also among them to
present himself before the
Lord." (Job 2:1)*

William Blake, the painter and poet (1757-1827),
created towards the end of his life a series of
paintings describing the story of Job. Geoffrey
Keynes, who together with Gwendolen Raverat
wrote the libretto for Ninette de Valois's *Job*,
believes that "there can be little doubt that [Blake]
saw in the story of Job a reflection of the spiritual
events of his own life." Ralph Vaughan Williams, the
composer, offered his *Job* to de Valois, stipulating
that it should not be danced "on points," as the
traditional balletic movement seemed to him
incapable of expressing the ideas of his Biblical
drama, which he did not call a "ballet" but rather, "A
Masque for Dancing," to point out his objection to a
balletic treatment.

De Valois based her choreography on the Blake
paintings, which provided her with a *mise en scène*.
Thus, she acquired a triple base: the Bible as seen
through Blake's eyes and Blake's paintings reflected
in Vaughan Williams's music, both forming the base
for her own creation.

The stage for the first production (for The
Camargo Society in London in 1931, designed by
Raverat) was divided into two planes. The rear
represented the heavenly sphere, with a staircase
leading to God's throne; the front part of the stage,
the earth, Job's homestead. The figure of God was
called in the program "Job's Spiritual Self," because,
as has already been mentioned, according to British
law at that time, depicting God on stage was a
punishable offense.

In the first scene Job, still a prosperous burgher, is
sitting with his wife and servants, whose many sons
and daughters dance before him as he blesses them.
In the following scene, heaven is empty and God's
throne deserted. Satan dances in mock adoration of
God and finally usurps the throne, and as he seats

himself on it there is a sudden blackout. Back on earth, Job's sons and their wives dance a tranquil minuet; when Satan enters suddenly, the dancers fall dead. In the next scene, Job's peaceful sleep is disturbed by Satan, War, Pestilence, and Famine. Messengers come to him with sad tidings of his offsprings' deaths and the loss of all his earthly possessions. Their dance is at first compassionate, but it changes into rebuke and anger, and Job rebels, cursing God. As he invokes God, Satan is revealed sitting on the heavenly throne. The role of Satan was danced in the original production by Anton Dolin and in the 1948 revival by Robert Helpmann.

Elihu, a young and beautiful man, enters and remonstrates Job, who perceives his error, and the heavens open again, revealing God enthroned. Satan again claims victory, but is repelled by "The Sons of Morning." Job's servants build an altar and worship God with musical instruments. Finally Job sits, a humbler but wiser man, his fortune and family restored — "So the Lord blessed the latter end of Job more than his beginning . . . he had also seven sons and three daughters . . . so Job died, being old and full of days . . . " (Job 42: 12-17).

De Valois's *Job*, together with her *Rake's Progress*, became a cornerstone of a special "British" style of ballet — a modern continuation of the narrative ballets of the Romantic era, emphasizing the psychological motives of the characters without recourse to the conventional mime of the old ballets, a line developed and brought to full fruition by Ashton and Tudor.

In 1975 Thames-TV planned a revival of de Valois's *Job* for an Easter broadcast. But she suggested a completely new choreography instead of

Jack Cole (standing), as Elihu, with Denishawn dancers in Ted Shawn's Job. (Photo: Dance Collection, Library and Museum of Performing Arts)

"Then was kindled the wrath of Elihu the son of Barachel the Buzite, of the kindred of Ram: against Job was his wrath kindled, because he justified himself rather than God . . . . " (Job 32:6, 8)

Robert North and Siobhan Davies, as Job and his wife, in the London Contemporary Dance Theatre production of The Story of Job, choreographed by Robert Cohan for Thames Television. (Photo: Courtesy of Thames Television)

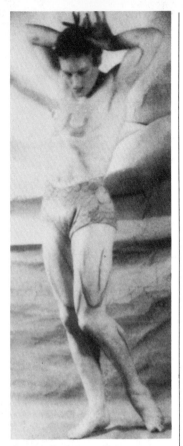

Anton Dolin, as Satan, in the original production of Ninette de Valois's Job. (Photo: Courtesy of Anton Dolin)

a reconstruction of her own work and Robert Cohan was commissioned to do the work. He, too, decided to use the magnificent Vaughan Williams music and base his ballet on the Blake paintings, but he used a modern dance movement vocabulary and used the possibilities offered by television techniques for creating effects of flying through space and revealing floor patterns never seen by the spectator in the theater.

Dancers of the London Contemporary Dance Theatre were used in the new work. Robert North filled both the role of Job and that of God, while Namron was Satan. (Casting a black dancer in the part of Satan triggered several sharp critical remarks.)

The tremendously strong visual designs of the Blake originals, such as the scene where Satan stands on the prostrated Job's abdomen when striking him with the boils, come across forcefully. Most effective are the (superimposed) figures of angels soaring through a myriad of stars, wheeling like a wreath of bodies through space.

The choreographer himself believes that lack of time and equipment prevented an even more faithful rendering of the Blake models. Still, the youthful, often quite bare, bodies of the dancers are in perfect accordance with the Blake originals. The modernity of the parable of Job is evident in this remarkable ballet, which succeeded in rendering abstract thought in concrete dance terms, which is perhaps one of the most typical aspects of the Old Testament storytelling technique.

Dancer-choreographer M[...]cus Schulkind in the titl[...] role of his modern work, [...] Job (1977), created to p[...] music by Randy Newma[...] (Photo: Nathaniel Tilest[...])

Paul Haakon, as the Bearer of Bad Tidings, in Ted Shawn's Job. (Photo: Dance Collection, Library and Museum of Performing Arts)

the profligate son

In 1812, Pierre Gardel, director of the Paris Opéra ballet school, created what can be regarded as the *Ur*-Prodigal Son, a ballet-pantomine in three acts called *L'enfant prodigue*. The father is called Reuben and is the head of a tribe, which lives in the vicinity of the Egyptian city Memphis, apparently prior to the Exodus. Act one takes place in a pastoral setting, the peasants preparing themselves for a festive sacrifice. Azaël, Reuben's son, is the prodigal who leaves his father's home, tired of the preferential treatment he believes his brothers receive. Azaël is attracted by the big town of Memphis — another country boy to be lured by city lights. On his way, the prodigal meets many adventures and finally returns home, sadder but wiser. Azaël, the prodigal, was danced by Auguste Vestris.

In his short story "The Stationmaster," Alexander Pushkin describes the post office, where the passengers wait to have the horses in their carriages changed. While the postmaster is busy with his accounts, the traveler looks at the pictures embellishing the walls of the modest dwelling. These are a set of prints telling the story of the Prodigal Son, with appropriate verses in German accompanying each engraving. The first picture shows an elderly man in a dressing gown and skullcap giving his impatient son a purse of money and blessing him. The second one is of the son's sinful life after he has left his father's house. He is shown at a table, surrounded by false friends and loose women. In the third picture the prodigal is in tatters, minding a herd of swine, his countenance sad. The last one is of the son's return, the old man still in his gown and cap, hurrying to welcome his returning offspring, while in the background a

Filius Prodigus (nineteenth-century German steel engraving). (The Bettmann Archive)

Kurt Jooss as the Father and Rolf Alexander as the Son in a 1946 performance of Jooss's Le fils prodigue (1931). (Photo: Dance Collection, Library and Museum of Performing Arts)

David Lichine in his Prodigal Son (1938) for Col. W. de Basil's Original Ballet Russe. (Photo: Dance Collection, Library and Museum of Performing Arts)

Anton Dolin, Leon Woizikovsky, and Serge Lifar (in the title role) in George Balanchine's original Prodigal Son (1929) for Diaghilev's Ballets Russes. (Photo: Dance Collection, Library and Museum of Performing Arts)

Anton Dolin in Lichine's Prodigal Son. (Photo: Nanette Kuehn, Dance Collection, Library and Museum of Performing Arts)

servant slaughters a fatted calf and the older brother is asking him the reason for the feast. This passage from Pushkin's story served as George Balanchine's inspiration when he was preparing his *Prodigal Son* for Diaghilev's company in 1929. Diaghilev was looking for something profound and deeply felt when he turned to the Biblical subject. Boris Kochno wrote the libretto and Serge Prokofiev was commissioned to compose the music. The New Testament tale (Luke 15:11-24) is, in Alexander Bland's opinion, a "heavy emotional story, redolent of Jewish Old Testament history, the antithesis of the cool and transparent lyricism of [Balanchine's] *Apollo.*"

Felia Doubrovska, as the Siren, in the premiere performance of Balanchine's **Prodigal Son;** *for Diaghilev's Ballets Russes, Théâtre Sarah Bernhardt, Paris, May 21, 1929. (Photo: Dance Collection, Library and Museum of Performing Arts)*

The Rouault sets and costumes designed for t Ballets Russes producti of the Balanchine work (seen clearly in photo at right) were revived for th New York City Ballet.

The Prodigal Son is a parable and as such poses a structural problem because, by its very nature, a parable falls into two parts, in the manner of an advertisement, namely "before" and "after" — and a dual structure tends to lose much of the dramatic tension as it bypasses the climax of a central part, act, or scene, when the dramatic change occurs. Balanchine solved this problem by staging a series of scenes, in the manner of a cartoon strip or picture book, or perhaps in what today would be termed a cinematic sequence built into three acts and danced without a pause.

Alexander Bland finds these, in turn, "straightforward" (the beginning); the orgy scene, in which the hero is seduced and stripped, influenced by modern, Expressionistic ("Central European") dance; the Prodigal's homeward voyage, "a cabaret turn"; and the finale, the son's homecoming, done "in the manner of silent film melodrama."

The actual rehearsals and preparation for the ballet at Monte Carlo are a story in their own right. Diaghilev had asked Georges Rouault to design the set, but the painter, though he attended rehearsals for several weeks, failed to produce any drawings. There are several versions of what finally took place. According to some, Diaghilev, worried about the situation, asked his chauffeur to take the painter on an "excursion," while he himself ransacked Rouault's hotel room and took with him the sketches he found. But Boris Kochno says that Diaghilev simply lost patience and told Rouault that a place had been reserved for him on next morning's train to Paris, not mentioning *The Prodigal Son* at all. The painter worked all night in his room, and before he left sent Diaghilev a bundle of sketches, from which the backdrops and costumes were made. The backdrops are in a style typical of Rouault, colors shining brightly from behind broad, black frame lines, reminding one of the stained glass windows of cathedrals.

It often happens in the theater that necessity is the best spark for originality, and several of the most interesting touches in Balanchine's work were the results of last minute crises. For example, most economical and convincing was the use of one single piece of practical stage prop, which serves in turn as a fence with gate, symbolizing the Prodigal's home, then becomes a banquet table, and later is stood upright as an abstract rostrum to be climbed on; it is turned upside down and becomes the ship on which the Prodigal sails, with the Siren who seduced him earlier forming the figurehead of the boat's prow.

Irina Baronova as the Si with Anton Dolin as the Prodigal, in David Lichi Prodigal Son (1938). (Photo: Dance Collecti Library and Museum of Performing Arts)

Balanchine's use of this long table as a boat, with the Siren's bright red cloak becoming a sort of sail with she herself part of the boat, was decided upon only at the dress rehearsal, as the "boat" which was to be used lay unfinished in the carpenter's workshop. The improvisation worked so well that it was kept. The idea of having the Prodigal's drinking mates in bald wigs was, as Balanchine himself states, "an afterthought," and the hairless pates add a most decadent, repulsive touch to the debauched revelries.

Balanchine, usually so cool and cerebral in his approach, chose to use acrobatic movement for certain scenes, such as when the Prodigal is seduced by the Siren, who wraps herself around his body like a snake and slithers down to the floor to lie at his feet, or when she is raised high on the shoulders of the dancers and looks down on the Prodigal who lies subdued, prostrated on top of the long table, or the moment when the table is stood on end with him clinging to the top, yards above the rest of the dancers, who hold the table up. For once, Balanchine allowed himself a moral judgment. Perhaps the ancient legend touched a deep, emotional layer concealed in everyone's soul, the point at which each man, whether he is successful and powerful or believes himself to be an utter failure, longs to return to the lost paradise of his childhood and his sheltered home. Everyone is, in some respects, a prodigal returning to his father. The "moral" of the legend is only one layer of its meaning.

Edwin Denby sees the *Prodigal Son* as, "told, since it is about good and evil, in two kinds of pantomime: the dry, insect-light insect-quick elegance and filth of atheism, and the fleshy Biblical vehemence — so Near Eastern and juicy — of sin and forgiveness, the bitter sin and sweet forgiveness. Still bolder as an image seems to me the leisure in the pacing of the scenes, which transport the action into a spacious patriarchal world, like a lifetime of faith."

The ballet of the Prodigal Son is a brilliant example of the multilayered charm the Bible story holds for modern audiences, quite apart from its religious content.

So are many other New Testament subjects treated by modern choreographers, such as Lazarus, the Mary episodes from Christ's life, and of course the Passion and the betrayal of Judas, all of which speak a universal language reaching beyond Christianity. Since the days when medieval passion plays brought together whole cities in sometimes three-day or even week-long pageants depicting the life and

Among the many dancer to perform the title role and that of the Siren, in George Balanchine's Pr igal Son (revived by the choreographer for his ow New York City Ballet in 1950) are Yvonne Moun and Francisco Moncion. (Photo: Roger Wood, Dance Collection, Libra and Museum of Perform Arts)

martyrdom of Christ, many choreographers have turned to the theme of Jesus in their work. Christian tradition does not preclude the portrayal of the Christ figure, at least not in connection with religious events. In modern times, untethered to church dogma, dances about episodes in Jesus's life have been created, with varying degrees of success. Recent examples include Barry Moreland's *Kontakion*, presented recently in London, in which the black American dancer William Louther was cast in the role of Jesus. In a dance duet by Paul Sanasardo, *Abandoned Prayer*, the relationship between Jesus and Judas is portrayed as a very complex one of love and dependence between two men. An electric lantern wielded in turn by each protagonist is an original device which turns the source of light into an inquisitorial tool, the intensity of the light not only illuminating the ties between the dancers but turning into the "third degree" projector shining into the face of the victim being interrogated. Sanasardo here uses light as a source of pain, suffering, and self-recognition.

On the other hand, Christ serves as a central figure in the works of Ross McKim and his small dance company called Moving Vision, which performs in churches in England. In 1973 the Mexican choreographer José Coronado premiered his *Danse Sacrée*, in which the Stations of the Cross are presented choreographically. The Spanish-Latin intensity of religious feeling and tradition has attracted a number of other modern dance creators as well, among them Anna Sokolow, José Limón, and Martha Graham. In *El Penitente*, Graham's Mexican mystery dance drama about a sect of

*A German engraving depicting **The Return of the Prodigal.** (The Bettmann Archive)*

*Jerome Robbins was the first to dance the title role when George Balanchine revived his **Prodigal Son** New York City Ballet in 1950. (Photo: George Pl Lynes, Dance Collection Library and Museum of Performing Arts)*

Woytek Lowski (alone and with the Idiots) in two scenes from the Boston Ballet production of Balanchine's **Prodigal Son.** *(Photo at far right: Harvey J. Segall)*

flagellants, she combines materials from the New and the Old Testaments by introducing the Fall of Man out of Genesis into scenes from Christ's life. In the twenty-fifth chapter of the Gospel according to Matthew, the kingdom of heaven is likened to ten virgins who took their lamps and went forth to meet the bridegroom. Five of them were wise, and five were foolish. Those who were foolish took their lamps but took no oil with them.

This parable, several times the source of inspiration for choreographers, stresses the preparation of the wise, who think of the future and the reckoning, and points out the dangers of sloth and of living only for the moment.

This idea occurs many times in the Old Testament as well as in the New Testament ("Watch therefore, for ye know neither the day nor the hour wherein the Son of man cometh." — Matthew 25:13).

Jean Börlin, who choreographed his *Les Vierges Folles* for the Ballet Suédois in 1920, was influenced by folk art from the Balecarlia region of Sweden. The libretto and music for his ballet were by Kurt Atterberg, the set and costumes by Einar Nerman. He used a folk song which begins:

And the heavenly kingdom resembles ten virgins,
Each of a different character.
Five are of indolent nature, their spirit idle and
    impure.
God pities the poor sinners!

Helgi Tomasson (as the
Prodigal Son) and a corps
of New York City Ballet
dancers (as the Idiots) in
Balanchine's Prodigal Son.
(Photo: Martha Swope)

As the catalogue of the Ballet Suédois, 1920-1925 exhibition, held at the Stockholm Museum of Dance in 1970, shows, the costumes were based on traditional folk costumes: The virgins wore wide green dresses with black stripes and high conical hats, and the lamps in their hands were flaming hearts. Börlin's version was a humorous one. Ninette de Valois used the same music for her *Wise and Foolish Virgins,* created for the Vic-Wells Ballet in 1933.

Frederick Ashton's approach to his *The Wise Virgins* — "one of the most beautiful Biblically derived ballets," as David Vaughan calls it — was quite different. As Ashton himself says in *The Dance Has Many Faces* (Columbia University Press, 1966), "In my ballet . . . which was arranged to the music of Bach, I went to eighteenth - century Baroque. . . . Whereas in *Leda and the Swan* I had studied the paintings, in this ballet I not only studied Baroque paintings in general, but also sculpture and architecture; and I tried to convey, with the bodies of the dancers, the swirling, rich elaborate contortions of the Baroque period. In this ballet, no lines were spiral, everything was curved and interlacing, and the line of the dancers was broken and tormented, so to speak."

The music for Ashton's *Wise Virgins* was arranged and orchestrated by William Walton; the sets and costumes were by Rex Whistler. The first performance of the work by the Sadler's Wells Ballet took place in April 1940, with Margot Fonteyn and Michael Somes in the principal parts. Whistler designed an elaborate set with pink walls, floral borders, and a golden, nail-studded door with two male angels, which corresponded with the intricate, asymmetrical groupings of Ashton's choreography. The critic for *Dancing Times* (May 1940) found "the music . . . delicately and sympathetically orchestrated . . . a delight to the ear . . . and the drop curtain and decor . . . a feast for the eye, the individual costumes . . . charming, but the mixture of periods a little confusing. The cherubs, for example, were Florentine, the bridegroom was reminiscent of 'Le Roi Soleil' and the bride's crown was pure Hollywood."

David Vaughan describes the work in his book, *Frederick Ashton and His Ballets* (London: A. & Ch. Black, 1977): "The ballet began with the mounting of an androgynous cherub guard before the gates — four dancers, one male, three female, all identically costumed in pink tights with short black velvet tunics decorated with stars. They were reinforced by a group of male angels, and the bride arrived with her parents, attended by the five wise

New York City Ballet's E ward Villella gave his firs performance as the Prodigal in Balanchine's Prodigal Son on January 1960. (Photo: Martha Swope)

virgins. The foolish virgins had a pert, tripping entrance, saucily led by Mary Honer. Fonteyn [as the bride] danced a solo that again was not in the least balletic in style — at the time it was said to be influenced by Hindu dancing."

The elegance of the sets, a certain daring extravagance (the women had flesh-colored tights and painted nipples showing through their draperies — as Vaughan points out), and the exquisite groupings all created a "show" which the dance critic of *Dancing Times* said reminded him of Diaghilev.

Ashton created his *Wise Virgins* during one of the darkest hours of World War II, less than a month before Hilter's armies overran Western Europe and Churchill replaced Chamberlain as Prime Minister. The lavish production was, perhaps, a gesture to cheer an English populace waiting for the German juggernaut to pounce. With today's hindsight, there seems to have been a moral to be gleaned from the parable about unpreparedness, with the foolish virgins representing "peace in our time," the slogan which was brandished by Chamberlain upon his return from Munich. But it is doubtful that such thoughts entered the minds of the audience while they admired Margot Fonteyn's dancing.

One of the dancers to as most recently the title role in Balanchine's **Prodigal Son** *is Mikhail Baryshnikov. (Photos: below, with company, Pierre Petitjean; right, Martha Swope)*

biblical dance and heritage

In a country where archaeology is a popular pastime and the Bible a book of national history, Biblical themes as reflected in works of art acquire a very special, concrete meaning. Therefore it is hardly surprising that Biblical dances created in modern Israel have specific connotations distinguishing them from others based on similar themes created by non-Israelis.

Dance creators turned naturally to the two sources available: to the folkloristic material found in Oriental Jewish communities of the Middle East and the surrounding Arab and Druse living traditions, and to the Bible, as a record of the past.

The Bible knows several forms of dance, but the actual information it offers about the dances performed by the Israelites is scant. In past centuries, scholars tried to research Biblical dancing, but without the help of pictorial evidence this was an impossible task. The third commandment precluded any visual evidence — "Thou shalt not make unto thee any graven image, or any likeness of any thing that is in heaven above or that is in the earth beneath . . . " (Exodus 20:4).

Paul Clarke and Patricia Ruanne, as the Prodigal and the Siren, in Barry Moreland's Prodigal Son (in ragtime) *for the London Festival Ballet. (Photo: Anthony Crickmay)*

" . . . a certain man had two sons: And the younger of them said to his father, 'Father, give me the portion of goods that falleth to me' . . . . And not many days after the younger son gathered all together, and took his journey into a far country, and there wasted his substance with riotous living." (Luke 15:11-13)

Barry Moreland's Prodigal Son (in ragtime) *for the London Festival Ballet is set in the twentieth century and features the ragtime music of Scott Joplin and Rockettes-like precision dancing by the corps. When the ballet premiered, the late Paul Clarke danced the role of the Prodigal. (Photo: Anthony Crickmay)*

"And when he had spent all, there arose a mighty famine in that land; and he began to be in want. I will arise and go to my father, and will say unto him, 'Father, I have sinned against heaven, and before thee, and am no more worthy to be called thy son . . . .'" (Luke 15:14, 18, 19)

" . . . be glad: for this thy brother was dead, and is alive again; and was lost, and is found." (Luke 15:32)

*Members of the Bat-Dor
Dance Company of Israel in
Domy Reiter-Soffer's I
Shall Sing to Thee in the
Valley of the Dead My Be-
loved (1971), a work which
interweaves the loves of
King David with the history
of the people of Israel.
(Photo: Mula & Haramaty)*

*"I have found David my ser-
vant . . . . My mercy will I
keep for him for evermore,
and my covenant shall
stand fast with him."
(Psalms 89:20, 28)*

*Jephthah's Daughter Co[ming] to Meet Her Father.
(Engraving: The Bettman[n] Archive)*

*" . . . Jephthah made thi[s]
vow to the Lord: 'If thou
wilt deliver the Ammoni[tes]
into my hands, then the
first creature that come[s]
out of the door of my ho[use]
to meet me when I retur[n]
from them in peace shal[l be]
the Lord's. I will offer th[is]
as a whole-offering.'"
(Judges 11:30-31)*

*"But when Jephthah cam[e]
to his house in Mizpah, [who]
should come out to mee[t]
him with tambourines a[nd]
dances but his daughter,
and she his only child; h[e]
had no other, neither so[n]
nor daughter." (Judges
11:34)*

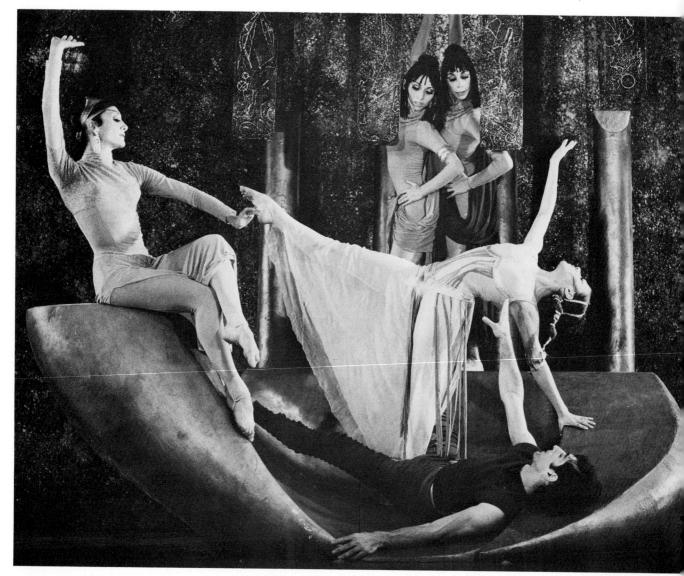

"And Miriam the prophetess, the sister of Aaron took a timbrel in her hand and all the women went after her with timbrels and with dances." (Exodus 15:20)

Rina Schoenfeld in the title role of her own work, Jephthah's Daughter, *for the Batsheva Dance Company. (Photo: Yaacov Agor)*

"When he saw her, he rent his clothes and said, 'Alas my daughter, you have broken my heart . . . . I have made a vow to the Lord, and I cannot go back.' She replied, 'Father . . . do to me what you have solemnly vowed . . . .'" (Judges 11:35-36)

Two gouaches, early 1900s:
Jephthah's Daughter and Her Companions, *and* **Jephthah's Daughter Dancing.** *(The Bettmann Archive)*

125

*Pearl Lang in her own S[...]
of Deborah (1959). (Pho[...]
Walter Strate)*

*"And Deborah, a proph-
etess, the wife of Lapido[...]
she judged Israel at that
time . . . and the childre[...]
Israel came up to her for
judgment." (Judges 4:4-[...]*

**Linda Hodes, as Deborah,
and Rina Schoenfeld, as
Jael, in the Batsheva Dance
Company production of
Pearl Lang's Tongues of
Fire. (Photo: Alex Benrod)**

*"That day Deborah and
Barak son of Abinoam sang
this song . . . 'Blest above
women be Jael, the wife of
Heber the Kenite; blest
above all women in the
tents.' . . . " (Judges 5:24)*

In the Biblical texts, the Hebrew terms *hul, pazez, karker, rakod,* and several others all point to different kinds of dance. But though the Bible tells us of triumph, dances of joy and dances of religious ecstasy, of dancing at festivals and weddings, all the evidence has to be evaluated by philological means alone. The texts mention leaps, skips and jumps, but still, we do not know what these saltations looked like.

The procession as the matrix from which dance is born has been described by researchers. Miriam celebrating the crossing of the Red Sea "took a timbrel in her hand; and all the women went out after her with timbrels and with dances . . . " (Exodus 15:20-21). David returning in triumph from his victory over the Philistines is met by women "singing and dancing" (1 Samuel 18:6). Jephthah's daughter came out to meet her father "with timbrels and with dances . . . " (Judges 11:34). But no one

Rina Nikova, the Russian-born and -trained dancer, settled in Jerusalem in 1925, founding the Biblical Ballet company there.

neteenth-century en-
ing which shows Miri-
(The Bettmann
ive)

"...d Miriam the proph-
...s, the sister of Aaron,
... a timbrel in her hand;
...all the women went out
... her with timbrels and
... dances."
...dus 15:20)

Sara Levi-Tanai's Jaakov in Horan, *for the Inbal Dance Company of Israel. (Photo: Mula & Haramaty)*

A Batsheva Dance Company production of Mos Efrati's treatment of the Cain and Abel story, Sin Lieth at the Door, with Schoenfeld, Ehud Ben-David, and Moshe Efrat (Photo: Mula & Haramat Courtesy of America-Isra Cultural Foundation)

The Bat-Dor Dance Company of Israel in Domy Reiter-Soffer's The Song of Deborah (1972), with Jeannette Ordman as Deborah. The ballet celebrates the victory of Israel over the armies of Sisera. (Photo: Mula & Haramaty)

knows what these dancing processions were like or what King David actually did when he was "dancing and leaping before the Lord" on bringing the Ark back, "with all his might" (2 Samuel 6:14-16). David was performing an ecstatic sacred dance, which his wife Michal, Saul's daughter — probably the first dance critic in history — did not like at all. Egyptian, Assyrian and other sources reveal little. So the recreators of Biblical dancing in modern Israel turned to living models and based their choreography on what they observed in Jewish and non-Jewish Oriental communities where folk dance tradition is still alive.

For thousands of years, since Biblical times, a Jewish community had existed in the southern tip of the Arabian Peninsula, in Yemen. The Yemenite Jews (who will henceforth be called simply Yemenites for the sake of brevity) possess a rich tradition of music and dance. This is deemed to be the best preserved, authentic ancient tradition extant. The isolation of this remote, scantily populated area of Arabia from the rest of the world and the separate, closed Jewish community of Yemen, which led its life quite apart from its Arab neighbors, preserved ancient forms of dance, ritual, and music, and kept them from foreign influences.

In 1925 a Russian-born and -trained ballerina, Rina Nikova, settled in Jerusalem, started a ballet school and founded a company called Biblical Ballet, which danced in Israel, and in the 1930s toured Europe, presenting its unique style, which was a strange mixture of classical ballet and Yemenite folk dance.

Nikova's dancers were Yemenite girls whose families had immigrated to the Holy Land at the beginning of the century. Daily, they received classical ballet training, and then the students would teach their teacher their own dances and rhythms, the material from which Nikova would choreograph her ballets. Traditionally, the Yemenite men are the dancers, but there exist also women's dances, and Nikova's students taught her both kinds of dance.

But the best known and most advanced and sophisticated Biblical ballets are those created by Sara Levi-Tanai, the founder and director of the Inbal Dance Theatre.

Levi-Tanai was born to Yemenite parents who settled in Israel about eighty years ago. The Bible, for Levi-Tanai, is an integral part of her and her nation's heritage, and she used themes and stories from the Old Testament for many of her dance works. One such work, her *Psalm of David* (1964), featured Margalit Oved in the leading role of

Anton Dolin in Keith Lester's David, Scene I Lester ballet was given premiere at Theatre Ro Newcastle-on-Tyne, England, on November 1935, with Dolin in the role. (Photo: Courtesy Anton Dolin)

134

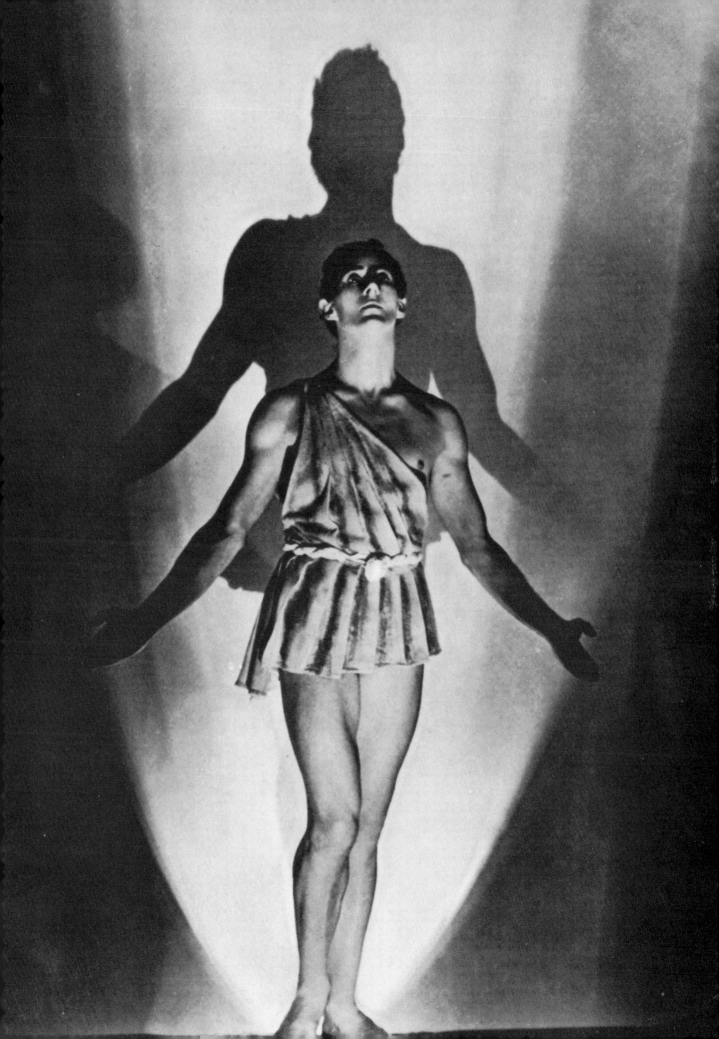

Anton Dolin in Scene VI
(left) and Scene II of
Keith Lester's David.
(Photos: Courtesy of
Anton Dolin)

*Ross Parkes and Barry
Smith in Martha Graham's
Point of Crossing (1975).
(Photo: Martha Swope)*

*"And he lighted upon a ce[r]
tain place . . . and lay dou[n]
in that place to sleep. An[d]
he dreamed, and behold [a]
ladder set up on the earth[,]
and the top of it reached [to]
heaven: and behold the
angels of God ascending
and descending on it."*
(Genesis 28:11-12)

Martha Graham's **The
Dream,** *with Ehud Ben-
David, Rena Gluck, and
Ohad Naharin. Graham
created this work, based on
the story of Jacob, for the
Batsheva Dance Company
in 1974. (Photo: Mula &
Haramaty)*

*Members of the Alvin Ai[...]
American Dance Theate[...]
two scenes from Ailey's
Three Black Kings: a ce[...]
bration (below) of Baltha[...]
the Black King of the
Nativity; and King Solo[...]
(right), danced by Clive
Thompson. (Photos: Loi[...]
Greenfield)*

Avishag, the girl brought to the aging monarch David to warm his shivering body.

In recent years Margalit Oved has been teaching and performing in California and has herself several times turned to Biblical subjects for her dances: for example, her *In the Beginning* for her own company or, four solos she choreographed and composed the music for, *The Mothers of Israel*, for Ze'eva Cohen.

In *Mothers*, Margalit used types of Yemenite women she knew in her childhood in Aden and her youth in Israel, and elevated the very realistic portraits to a general level lending Sarah, Rebecca, Rachel, and Leah a preciseness of everyday, purposeful movement, as they each in turn go about their household chores and nevertheless attain a symbolic elevation.

In this task she was greatly helped by the fact that Ze'eva Cohen herself is of Yemenite stock. This realism is possible only with artists who can perceive the mythical matriarchs of their nation as part of contemporary life, seeing themselves as a continuation of the Biblical past. When one compares two modern ballets, created nearly at the same time about the same subject, namely Jacob (incidentally also at the same place, in Tel Aviv), by two great artists, Martha Graham and Sara Levi-Tanai, the difference of approach becomes clear.

In both cases the symbolic materials are the same. In both, Jacob's dream is pivotal; in both there is his struggle with the angel; there are Rachel and Leah, his two wives (compressed by Graham into one figure). But for Levi-Tanai, Jacob accepts his destiny as leader and father of his nation after his struggle with God's messenger. While for Graham, it is acceptance of each man's individual destiny by

Ze'eva Cohen in Mothers of Israel, a four-part work created for her by Margalit Oved which deals with four Biblical women: Sarah, Rebecca, Rachel, and Leah. (Photo: Lois Greenfield)

Jacob's Vision

"And Jacob went fr(Beersheba . . . and he lighted upon a certain place . . . and he took t(stones of that place, an(put them for his pillow(. . . . And he dreamed, (behold a ladder set up (the earth, and the top o(reached to heaven; and (hold the angels of God (cending and descendin(it." (Genesis 28:10-12)

himself. The visual and conceptual differences between Graham's *The Dream* (created for Batsheva in 1974) and Levi-Tanai's *Jacob* (Inbal, 1973) are clear. In *Jacob* the struggle with the angel is a solo in which the young Jacob struggles with the burden of destiny quite early in the fifty-minute work, the presence of the angel reflected only in his own movement. In *The Dream* he has to wrestle with a figure which descends from the shimmering ladder. The angel brings with him an oblong object, reminiscent of the *hoshen*, a symbolic ornament the High Priest wore on his breast, to bestow Jacob's destiny upon him. While Graham took many liberties with the narrative, such as making his two wives into one "Woman," Levi-Tanai stayed closer to the original story. Both choreographers endowed props with symbolic meaning.

The sets and costumes were designed by the two leading scenic artists of Israel, Dani Karavan for Graham and David Sharir for Inbal, and they reflect the two distinctly different approaches. Sharir's costumes were mostly brown and beige with white and black ornaments, very detailed, with the texture of a weave of ribbons. A circle of rounded stones is the well where Jacob meets his future wife; it provides the stone upon which he rests his head, and it serves in all the scenes until his journey back with his tribe to his fatherland, when the stones are carried by the girls, who are riding on the boys' shoulders as if on the backs of camels.

Karavan also used sculpted stones, but they are nearly white and have clear straight edges; the most important piece of his set is the heavenly ladder, made of metal, with wires that scintillate and sparkle attached to its sides.

Israel is the only country in the world where the Bible is an almost concrete, even realistic presence. Its message is specific, geared to the Israeli nation's history, destiny, past, and present. As such it presents the Israeli artist with problems which a gentile choreographer does not have to solve.

José Limón (kneeling right) and Lucas Hoving (center) in Limón's The Traitor (1954). (Photo: Matthew Wysocki)

"Then one of the twelve, called Judas Iscariot, went unto the chief priests. And said unto them, 'What will ye give me, and I will deliver him unto you?' And they convenanted with him for thirty pieces of silver."
(Matthew 26:14-15)

en in José Limón's The
itor are (left) Clay Talia-
o and (right) Christo-
r Gillis and Mark Am-
rman. (Photos: Martha
ope)

"Then Judas . . . repented
himself . . . Saying, 'I have
sinned in that I have be-
trayed the innocent blood'
. . . . And he cast down the
pieces of silver . . . and
went and hanged himself."
(Matthew 27:3-5)

José Limón and company
in Limón's The Traitor
(1954). (Photo:
Matthew Wysocki)

Constantine

conclusion

The rich tapestry of Biblical dance, covering many countries and centuries, is, by its very nature, a survey of dramatic content expressed in dance terms. Perhaps it is also a contribution to the discussion about whether there is a place for ballet dramaturgy in modern dance at all.

Personally, I do not believe that any art form which uses the human body as its material can be devoid of dramatic content, whether it is as abstract as Cunningham's or that of a Petipa reconstruction. The meeting or parting of people, embrace or

...nes Truitte of the Lester ...ton Dancers in the title ...e of Alvin Ailey's Accord- ...to St. Francis (1954). ...oto: Constantine)

The Alvin Ailey American Dance Theater in Ailey's Three Black Kings (1976). (Photo: Lois Greenfield)

repulsion, every fall or leap carries an emotional, dramatic message, whether the creator intended this or not. The use of external material — literary, religious, psychological, or philosophical — adds a dimension and a term of reference to the pure movement material. The Bible, as such, is a grid in which choreographers can place their work.

Why is the Bible such a rich source of inspiration, apart from the fact that it offers many "good stories" and forms for many people a deep layer of childhood memories?

Helmut Scheier, a German dance critic who studied theology before turning to ballet, thinks this has to do with the special way in which the Old Testament expresses abstract ideas in concrete, dramatic situations. He finds that, in the Bible, the narrative often serves higher moral or philosophical purpose without becoming didactic. For this reason, Biblical themes lend themselves easily to choreography, which is also an art endeavoring to express ideas in concrete terms of moving bodies in a theatrical situation.

It is impossible to describe here completely the panorama of Biblical dance. Often the Biblical basis of a dance work is hidden beneath many layers of stylization — or it may disappear in the course of the work's development, becoming a foundation concealed by the building it supports. For example, watching Jiri Kylián's *Stoolgame* (Nederlands Dans Theater), one is aware of the social content of his cruel game of musical chairs. But as the choreographer himself told me, the basic idea he started with was the Jesus-Judas-Mary situation, the love-and-betrayal New Testament story. Armed with this information, one can discover the Biblical infrastructure in the choreography. The duets between the two male protagonists acquire a new meaning; the role of the central female dancer becomes more specific, and the final turning of the stools upside down, which become candelabra placed round the dead body laid out on the table, a pietà. Actually, the table surrounded by stools was the Biblical image of the Last Supper from which Kylián embarked on his choreographic voyage, which took him into another area altogether.

It is quite surprising that an artist such as Kylián, who was educated in Communist Prague where the Bible is not taught in the schools, should turn to a New Testament subject in the first place. In fact, it points out the many ways in which the Bible permeates our culture, is the yeast in the dough of Western art, and is so deeply interwoven in our lives and thought that we hardly notice it unless we examine closely our very existence. □

Rudolf Nureyev in Martha Graham's El Penitente. (Photo: Linda Vartoogian)

giora manor

Editor of the Israel Dance *annual, Giora Manor is an Israeli correspondent for European and American dance publications, including* Dance Magazine, *and is the editor of the arts section of* Al-Hamishmar. *Born in Prague, Czechoslovakia, and a member of kibbutz Mishmar Haemek, Giora Manor worked for many years in Israel as a theater director before becoming a journalist and dance critic.*

about this book

DANCEBOOKS Number Two, *The Gospel According to Dance,* is the second volume in a series of books produced at Dance Magazine and covering various areas of instruction and interest in the field of dance. This volume was published and distributed by St. Martin's Press, Inc., 175 Fifth Avenue, New York, New York 10010.

Previously published: *Pas de Deux: A Textbook on Partnering* by N. Serebrennikov, adapted by Marian Horosko, translated by Elizabeth Kraft.

Editor-in-Chief **William Como**
Executive Editor **Richard Philp**
Art Director **Herbert Migdoll**
Assistant Art Director **Deborah Thomas**
Production Director **June L. Thomas**
Production Editor **James Kreydt**
Assistant Editor **Joan Pikula**
Editorial Assistant **Mary Day**
Cover Design **Paul Gamarello**
Cover Photo **Jack Vartoogian**

On the cover: A scene from Alvin Ailey's masterwork, *Revelations,* a ballet depicting American black response to Biblical themes. Clive Thompson (in foreground) and members of the Alvin Ailey American Dance Theater capture the vigor and spiritual commitment with which "the living" Old and New Testaments often are portrayed. (Photo: Jack Vartoogian)

bibliography

Allan, Maude. ***My Life and Dancing.*** London: Everett & Co., 1908.

Amrad, Esther. "The Procession as a Source of Dance." ***Israel Dance,*** 1977, p. 20.

Bland, Alexander (pseud.). ***The Nureyev Image.*** London: Studio Vista, 1967.

Charbonnel, Raoul. ***La Danse.*** Paris: Garniére Fréres, (1900?).

Denby, Edwin. ***Dancers, Buildings and People in the Streets.*** New York: Horizon Press, 1965.

Devrient, Eduard. ***Geschichte der Deutschen Schauspielkunst.*** 2 volumes. Münich-Wien: Langen-Müller, 1976.

Flemming, Willi. "Geschichte des Jesuitentheaters." ***Schriften der Gesellschaft für Theatergeschichte,*** Volume 32. Berlin, 1923.

Gregor, Joseph. ***Kulturgeschichte des Ballets.*** Zurich: Scientia-Verlag, 1946.

Hartnoll, Phyllis, ed. ***The Oxford Companion to the Theatre.*** London and New York: Oxford University Press, 1951.

Haskell, Arnold. ***Balletomania.*** London: Victor Gollancz, 1934.

Ingber-Brin, Judith. "The Russian Ballerina and the Yemenites." ***Israel Dance,*** 1975, p. 19.

Jelizaveta, Suricová. "Sovetsky balet v prvních letech po Rijnové Revoluci." ***Tanecní*** Listy. Prague: November, 1977, p. 7.

Kessler, H. Graf. and Von Hofmannsthal, H. ***Josephslegende.*** Berlin and Paris: A. Furstner, 1914.

Keynes, Geoffrey. ***Blake.*** London: Faber & Faber, 1949.

Kindermann, Heinz. ***Theatergeschichte Europas.*** Salzburg: O. Muller, 1959.

Kochno, Boris. ***Diaghilev and the Ballets Russes.*** New York: Harper & Row, 1970.

Lenneman, Heinz. "Der Tanz der Salome." ***Die Waage.*** Stolberg/Rhld., Chemie Grüenthal 15/1976, p. 121.

Lifar, Serge. ***Ma Vie.*** New York and Cleveland: World Publishing Company, 1965.

Manor, Giora. ***Inbal — Quest for a Movement Language.*** Tel-Aviv: "Tavnit., Press. Ltd., 1975.

Manor, Giora. ***The Life and Dance of Gertrud Kraus.*** Tel-Aviv: Kibbutz Hamevhad Publishing House, 1978.

McDonagh, Don. ***The Complete Guide to Modern Dance.*** New York; Doubleday, 1976.

Michel, Artur. "Salome and Herodias, from the Bible to Martha Graham." ***Dance Magazine,*** February, 1946, p. 8; and March, 1946, p. 18.

Mueller, Johannes. "Das Jesuitendrama." ***Schriften zur Deutschen Literatur,*** Volume 7, 1930.

Oesterly, W.O.E. ***The Sacred Dance.*** New York: Dance Horizons, 1923.

Roslavleva, Natalia. ***Era of the Russian Ballet.*** London: Victor Gollancz, 1966.

Shawn, Ted. ***Dance We Must.*** London: Dennis Dobson, 1946.

Siegel, Marcia. ***At the Vanishing Point.*** New York: Saturday Review Press, 1972.

Slonimsky, Yuri, et al. ***The Soviet Ballet.*** New York: Da Capo Press, 1970.

Staub, Shalom. "Just an Echo? The Dances of Yemenite Women." ***Israel Dance,*** 1976, p. 154.

Staub, Shalom. "A Man Has Brains Until He Gets Up to Dance." ***Israel Dance,*** 1975, p. 15.

Vuillier, Gaston. ***A History of Dancing.*** Paris: Hachette, 1898.

Warren, Larry. ***Lester Horton.*** New York: Marcel Dekker, 1977.

Warren, Larry, et al. "Lester Horton's Dance Theatre." ***Dance Perspectives*** No. 31, 1967.